Gayle's Legacy

Gayle's Legacy

Recipes, Hints and Stories Culled from a Lifelong Relationship with Food

REVISED EDITION

GAYLE COATES WIGGLESWORTH

To order additional copies of this book, contact:
Xlibris Corporation
1-888-795-4274
www.Xlibris.com
Orders@Xlibris.com
20181

CONTENTS

MUNCHIES AND NOSHES

SOUPS AND SALADS

VEGETABLES AND SIDE DISHES

MAIN COURSES

THE PUD (DESSERTS)

EMMA'S SECRETS

ILLUSTRATIONS

Foreword

Currently frozen prepared products and "take out" food make up the bulk of our meals, yet people still have a psychological need to get in the kitchen and get their hands covered with flour. More and more people want to be able to cook but have less time for practice and less exposure to techniques—unless you count watching the cooking shows on Saturday television.

I come from the generation that learned to cook and can cook with minimal effort, having honed my skills through the years. But my children, my colleagues at work and many of my friends do not have these skills and are always lamenting the fact. Repeated requests for directions to make something or another and lavish praise for simple dishes finally pushed me into action. Thus this book started to grow.

Anyone who likes good food can cook and this book is going to teach you how. I have gathered the recipes I used, the ones my mother, my family and my friends passed on to me. I wrote down the recipes for those favorite dishes which resided only in my head. And I have included recipes from the people who brought dishes to contribute to the rituals, gatherings and special occasions at my house. These recipes are part of the memories of my life.

I wrote detailed instructions on how to prepare each dish as the shortcuts and modifications are what beginners struggle with and accomplished cooks do without thinking. I am constantly amazed at how easy it is to cook when its all written down in front of you.

And the last section of the book is made up of Emma's recipes. Emma Lewis Mohney was my maternal grandmother, who died before I or any of my brothers and sisters were born. She kept a little brown notebook filled with recipes. My mother cherished that book and used it until her own death. By then it was brittle with age and spills, the ink was faded and the writing hard to decipher. All of us wanted the book so in a moment of craziness I took it and promised to copy the recipes for everyone. The months following that rash promise turned into years, and my guilt tugged at me. So while the ideas were jelling about this cook book, I thought I would add Emma's.

Emma's section does not include detailed instructions on how to assemble her recipes because there were none. In that day, it was assumed everyone knew the basic rules for canning, candy making and baking. Additionally, the measurements are vague, a tablespoon was not the measuring kind, it was the eating kind, so there were differing sizes, thus instructions like a scant cup or a heaping teaspoon. They also used comparisons such as lard the size of an egg. What sized were their eggs? And flour to make a stiff batter? But what this really tells you is that you don't have to be an exacting scientist to be a good cook. After all thousands of people cooked for years with a pinch of this or a handful of that and were able to turn out successful meals. Of course when the diners have been working all day in the fields and there was no other place to eat they were probably a little forgiving if the cake was heavy or the cookies soggy.

I believe every cook should own two standard cookbooks. I recommend The Joy of Cooking and Better Homes and Gardens New Cookbook. These books, or ones similar, not only carry a wide variety of recipes but they contain tables for conversion of ounces to cups, emergency substitutions of ingredients and basic information everyone needs but no one can remember. My cookbook does not do those things. It is only meant to provide you with those tasty, different recipes that become family favorites. These recipes can be described as comfort food, the smells, tastes and textures remind you of other times and places. Even the "In" restaurants are turning to this kind of food to attract clientele.

I designed the cookbook to be handy to use in your kitchen, and I left space for your notes and modifications as I know the more you cook the more changes you'll make. Write them down for the next time you use the recipe and later for your children's benefit. Once you start using this cookbook its meant to become yours, it will no longer be mine.

Happy Cooking,
Gayle Coates Wigglesworth

Addendum

Five years have passed since I distributed this book to close family and friends and of course, a lot has happened in our family. First of all, my husband and I moved to Houston, Texas so I could take a position with a large Mortgage Company. That was a major change for the entire family. No more would we be having those large traditional family gatherings at our house.

After the first year we were gone Diane and Miles stepped up to the plate and agreed to host the Thanksgiving get-togethers. And since they had already received their copy of Gayle's Legacy, Diane proclaimed she was just going to go by the book, and they did. And still do. So now we go to California to their house to gather at a different Wigglesworth house on Thanksgiving.

Both of our daughters married since we left California and their husbands are a great addition to the family. Additionally both new son-in-laws cook and do it well.

Our oldest son, Mitch and his wife Nikki, have moved to Phoenix and are happily ensconced in a whole new life.

And of course friends and other family have relocated and all the grandchildren are growing like weeds. But that's life, full of changes. That's what makes it fun.

The changes I've made to this book reflect many of these changes in our lives but the essence is the same, just as the family is the same. After all, family is family.

Gayle Coates Wigglesworth
March, 2003

Gayle's Legacy

*The new Wigglesworth family on August 1, 1981 with
Miles, Dave, Mitch, Janet and Marc in the back row,
Gayle and Danielle in front*

Meet the Cook

I learned to cook early. My sister and I were baking cakes when we were six and seven years old. She could read the simple recipes for us by then. During our high school years my mother took a job and worked 11:00 a.m. to 8:00 p.m. so my sister and I took over the preparation of the nightly meals for about a year. I think that was the time we became cooks. In our family a dinner included a main dish, a starch (usually potatoes), a vegetable, a salad, and a desert. And because we did the shopping every Saturday we had to plan, buy and then cook within the allocated budget. True, we frequently served meals like pizza, minute steaks and tuna casseroles. And we made some major mistakes. Trying to be creative we tried many a deviation, catsup cookies—bad. Pigs in a Blanket were loved by everyone but me. I should have listened to the family on that one because seven years later an identical recipe won the Pillsbury Cook Off. At any rate it was a wonderful testing ground for fledgling cooks. And my father was appreciative enough of our efforts to be complementary no matter how we provoked his sensitive stomach. Our brothers would eat anything to get dessert and my mother ate at work so didn't witness the disasters. Although, looking back I realize she probably knew about them.

When my mother took back the cooking responsibility I still helped because by that time I was cooking with ease. And with my mother available for consultations I no longer had disasters of any magnitude.

As a young woman I moved to San Francisco where I knew no one. It was my Great Adventure. I was very poor for many years, as were most of my friends, so we cooked each other cheap meals, and drank jug wine and didn't understand that we were deprived. Later after my daughter was born, my cooking became a harried effort to get a nutritious meal on the table every day economically and quickly between work and bedtime. It was during those years an extended family evolved. It consisted of friends who shared special occasions and holidays with us. Those holiday feasts were continuations of the joyous celebrations I knew as a child, surrounded by family and friends.

My daughter was ten when I met and married Dave. He had been the chief chef in his family for about eight years by that time. I said I married him because he cooked like my mother. They were both artists with leftovers. Skilled leftover cooks turn out meals that can never be duplicated but can surprise and delight the diners. The occasional disaster only emphasize the successes and become funny stories to recount in the years to come.

When we were first married Dave did all the weekly cooking. Oh how delightful to come home from work to a house filled with wonderful smells. I took my turn producing Sunday dinner. All the kids, Grandma and occasionally other relatives and friends showed up for Sunday dinner. It was tradition. I had fun with these meals, fixing old favorites and trying new ones, reveling in having an appreciative, hungry audience once again.

Over the intervening years the cooking responsibility has changed and continues to change along with the needs and the traditions of the family. My husband and I cook together or, depending on the menu, we take turns. And now the kids and their families frequently participate in big dinners by bringing part of the meal or preparing some of the meal at our house. In fact last Thanksgiving, for twenty-five people, wouldn't have been possible if everyone hadn't helped. None of us wanted to spend the entire day in the kitchen and be too exhausted to enjoy the dinner. Sharing the pride of good cooking, setting up and taking down of the table, as well as the eating meant enjoyment for everyone.

This cookbook is the history of my family. It could be any family. I invite you to share it and become a part of the family.

The Art of Leftovers

I've heard many a person announce haughtily that they don't eat leftovers. I can only sympathize with their self-imposed limitations. They are missing some of the best meals available. I suppose my mother became a leftover queen out of necessity. She didn't have the money to feed the whole family a fresh meal every night. She bought the week's groceries on Saturday, which was always hamburger and hot dog night. Friday was a meatless night, Thursday was leftovers from the entire week, which sometimes included leftover leftovers. So Sunday through Wednesday had to have meals prepared from scratch or previous meals.

My husband, Dave, was also a wonder with leftovers because during those years after he lost his wife he was making meals for his four kids and he had to face eating the meal a second time or reusing the ingredients. He couldn't see wasting food so he used his imagination. Both of these people were great cooks.

The art of leftovers is to turn the remaining pieces of one or more previous meals into another meal that doesn't even resemble the first. Yes, I always need one more meal from the Thanksgiving fixings. I never have enough on the holiday but after that second meal you have to use some imagination to finish up the turkey. Remember with freezers available it doesn't have to be eaten the same week. Suppose you served roasted chicken, mashed potatoes, gravy and vegetables for dinner on Sunday. On Wednesday you could cut up the chicken, combine it with gravy and vegetables and put it in a casserole dish. Cover it with the mashed potatoes and bake it until the potatoes are brown on top and the rest is bubbly. Or stick this casserole in the freezer and get it out a few weeks later, it will be just as good and oh, so easy. It makes my mouth water thinking about it.

Given this scenario, doesn't it make sense to cook just a little more than you'll eat at the meal and get a second meal from the first? And if you don't have enough for a meal, freeze the leftovers and accumulate them to throw into soup or a rice dish such as Jambalaya or Paella.

Many of the recipe's from this book can be made from leftovers and I'm giving you a list to help you locate one for you to try.

Cooked Chicken? Try:

Turkey Puffs
Chinese Chicken Salad
Spinach Salad
Chinese Fried Rice
Dave's Rice Pilaf
Chicken Kung Poa
Chicken Fettuccini
Gayle's Jambalaya Rice
Paella
Sweet and Sour Chicken
Turkey Tortilla Casserole

Cooked Turkey? Try:

Turkey Puffs
Spinach Salad
Dave's Rice Pilaf
Chicken Fettuccini
Gayle's Jambalaya Rice
Paella
Turkey Mole
Turkey Tortilla Casserole

Cooked roasted beef or pot roast? Try:

Beef Stroganoff

Gayle's Black Bean Chili
Tamale Pie

Cooked ham? Try:

Turkey Puffs
Spinach Salad
Chinese Fried Rice
Crustless Quiche
Gayle's Mac and Cheese
Gayle's Jambolaya Rice
Paella
Quiche
Scalloped Potatoes

Cooked pork? Try:

Turkey Puffs
Spinach Salad
Chinese Fried Rice
Crustless Quiche
Gayle's Black Bean Chili
Gayle's Jambalaya Rice
Paella
Quiche
Sweet and Sour Chicken
Tamale Pie

Use your imagination, what to you have to lose?

Menus and Meals

One of the most difficult skills for cooks to learn is how to turn a bunch of recipes into memorable meals. It takes time and practice to get all the pieces and parts together at the right time. The first couple of times I served Yorkshire Pudding with the roast beef I thought I was going to have a nervous break down. No matter how many times we have these dinner someone always decides to go to the bathroom or get their drink refreshed just when I'm trying to get the pudding out of the oven and on to the table before it sinks.

If you're new at this, start with simple menus where some of the dishes can be prepared prior to meal time, this gives you a chance to concentrate on the complicated dishes.

Choosing all the components for the meal is important. Not only do you want a selection from all the food categories but you want them to enhance each other. I, personally, require a color variety. For instance, I don't want all my dishes to be yellow or white. I like my meals made up from dishes where the color, the textures and the tastes compliment each other.

I've listed some of our family's favorite menu's as a sample for your planning. Thanksgiving at our house will include all the items on the following menu, and we might even add something to that menu but we have never successfully been able to remove one item.

All of the recipes on the menu marked with an asterisk will be in this book.

Thanksgiving at our House:

Thanksgiving Turkey on the Barbeque with Gravy *
Cornbread and Oyster Stuffing *

Cranberry Cherry Relish*
Mashed Potatoes*
Candied Sweet Potatoes*
Connie's Strawberry Jello Mold*
Peas
Corn
Sherrill's Yeast Rolls*
Pumpkin Pie*
Chocolate Pie

Easter Brunch at our House:

Baked Ham
Quiche (Lorraine and Green Chili)*
Smoked Salmon
Cream Cheese
Assorted Cheeses
Fresh Vegetable and Relish Tray
Deviled Eggs
Fresh Fruit Salad* or Five Cup Salad*
Gayle's Signature Green Salad*
Basket of Assorted Breads
Easter Eggs and Candies on the center piece
Blueberry Cheesecake*

A Popular Birthday Dinner:

Pot Roast*
Mashed Potatoes*
Yorkshire Pudding*
Pear and Blue Cheese Salad* or Spinach Salad*
Green Beans* or Fresh Peas
Birthday Cake of Choice

A Summer Barbeque:

Teriyaki Chicken*
Rice Pilaff a la Dave*
Gayle's Signature Green Salad*
Cukes and Onions in Sour Cream*
Sour Dough Bread and Butter
Vanya's Strawberry Dream Cake*

An Elegant Company Dinner:

Cheese Puffs*
Pate and Assorted Cheeses with Crackers
Pear and Blue Cheese Salad* or Gayle's Signature Green
*   Salad * with the shrimp omitted*
Paella*
Crescent Dinner Rolls*
Carmel Apple Bread Pudding*

A Party Buffet:

Gayle's Black Bean Chili*
Chopped Onions, Grated Cheese and Tortilla Chips
Turkey Puffs*
Broccoli Salad*
Relish Tray, including fresh vegetables
Green Chili and Cheese Casserole*
Connie's Strawberry Jello Mold*
2 or 3 Sweet Breads from the freezer (Persimmon, Zuchinni,
*   Apricot, Friendship or Banana)**

Let's Talk Cheese

Cheese is used in recipes for many reasons and if you don't think about how you are using it, you will abuse it.

Remember that cheese if full of calcium and protein but it also contains fat and cholesterol. Sometimes cheese is the dominant flavor in a dish, such as in macaroni and cheese or a quiche and sometimes it is only added for texture or binding or an additional subtle flavor to a dish such as lasagna.

NEVER use cheap or inferior cheese in a recipe when the cheese dominates. If you can't afford a good cheese for these dishes, cook something else. I favor Swiss, Jarlsberg, Vermont Cheddar or a good orange Cheddar for quiches but I never mix one of the Swiss cheeses with a Cheddar as the flavors only fight each other. Mix any of them with a milder cheese such as a Jack to tone down the flavor or extend the expensive cheese.

I always use low fat cottage cheese instead of ricotta, I can't tell the difference and if I have more than I need in the carton I like to eat the cottage cheese. If you're bothered by the difference in texture between the two cheeses, put the cottage cheese in the food processor and blend it as smooth as ricotta.

I always grate my cheese in the food processor. One pound gives you approximately three cups of grated cheese. After I grate it I put it in Baggies for the freezer. That way I don't have to do the grating the same time I'm doing the cooking. It makes my life simpler. I just take the appropriate cheese from the freezer, let it set for a couple of hours use what I want, reseal it and freeze it again. If I'm just using it for topping I don't bother defrosting, I chip off enough for what I want, let that set a few minutes then crumble it on top of my salad or casserole.

I don't freeze snack cheese with one exception. We all love a soft blue cheese, our favorite is Blue Castillo, which we buy in hunks and keep in the freezer. But don't worry, one is always ready in the cheese drawer of the refrigerator. This is the cheese we love in our salads, spread on picnic sandwiches and just eat on celery or crackers. Other versions include a creamy blue brie from France and Gorgonzola from Italy.

I very seldom use Parmesan cheese anymore preferring to buy aged Asiago and grate it myself. Because this is a fairly dry cheese I can use it straight from the freezer with no defrosting. I like the flavor much better than Parmesan.

Notes:

Cookies, Candies and Baked Goods

Sunday dinner at our House in 1994.
Grandchildren Gage (Marc's son), Nicole and Amy
(Miles' children) with our son Marc

CONTENTS

Apricot Bread

Ever feel the need to bake on a cold dismal Saturday? Try this recipe. I bake it in a fluted pan or a pudding mold. It's wonderful straight from the oven or put part of it in the freezer for that time when unexpected company arrives.

What you need:

1 ½ cups dried apricots cut into bite size pieces
½ cup hot water
1 cup sugar
2 tablespoons butter
1 egg
3/4 cup orange juice
2 cups flour
2 teaspoons baking powder
1/4 teaspoon baking soda
1 teaspoon salt
1 cup chopped nuts

How to assemble:

Pour the hot water over the apricots and let set until they're cool
In a large bowl mix the butter, sugar and egg together
Stir in orange juice
In another bowl mix together flour, salt, baking powder and baking
    soda
Combine the contents of both bowls
Add the nuts, apricots and the water the apricots are setting in
Mix thoroughly

Pour into two greased loaf or flute pans
Let set for 20 minutes to rest
Bake in a preheated oven at 350° for approximately 50 minutes or
until a toothpick inserted in the middle comes out clean.

Notes:

Aunt Kate's Brownies

Aunt Kate was my dad's sister. When I was living in San Francisco, Aunt Kate and her husband Phil used to stay with me when they traveled between my folks in Southern California and three of their kids, who had moved to Oregon. We got to be good friends over the years and when they moved to Oregon we visited them many times.

I don't know where she got this recipe but she gave it to me in the '70's. I made the mistake of making them for a friend, who is a chocolat-a-holic. One night she called me at 3:00 a.m. for the recipe. It's that kind of brownie.

What you need:

Brownie:
9 x 13 baking pan, sprayed with PAM
1 cup white sugar
1 cube (½ cup) of softened butter or margarine
4 eggs
1 cup flour
1 16oz can of Hersey's chocolate syrup
1 cup of coarsely chopped nuts (optional)

Icing:
1 ½ cups white sugar
6 tablespoons of softened butter or margarine
6 tablespoons of milk
1 cup of semi-sweet chocolate chips (8oz)
½ teaspoon of vanilla

How to assemble:

Brownie:
Cream the butter and sugar together to start the brownies
Add the eggs and beat
Stir in the flour
Add the Hershey's syrup and mix well
Add the walnuts
Pour in the prepared baking pan
Bake for 30 to 35 minutes at 350°
Remove from oven and cool in pan
While the brownies are cooling begin the icing:

Icing:
Place sugar, butter and milk in a 1 ½ quart sauce pan and bring to
    a boil
Boil one minute stirring constantly
Remove from the flame
Beat in the chocolate chips and the vanilla
Continue beating until mixture is creamy
Pour over pan of warm brownies and spread evenly
Let cool until frosting sets
Serve

Notes:

If these last long enough they freeze beautifully.

Barb's Peanut Butter Cookies

My cousin, Barb, was a favorite of my parents and when she moved to California in the mid 50's, they were delighted. Over the years she has been more like an older sister than a cousin. I baby-sat for her kids when I was in high school just as she had for us in Michigan when she was a teenager. Shortly after I moved to San Francisco, she moved to Newcastle, up in the California Gold Country. I spent many a weekend with her family just as she had spent time with mine when she first moved away from home.

Barb made these cookies for her family. Maybe I like them because they're not ice box cookies like most peanut butter cookies are. When I get ready to bake I have little patience for waiting for the dough to chill. But the best reason to use this recipe is the peanut butter flavor, try it and you'll see what I mean.

What you need:

1 cup brown sugar (tightly packed)
1 cup white sugar
1 cup cooking oil
1 cup peanut butter
2 eggs
2 ½ cups flour
2 teaspoons soda
½ teaspoon salt

How to assemble:

Cream sugars, oil and peanut butter together
Add eggs and continue to mix

Add baking soda and salt to flour and add slowly to mixture
Mix well
Drop from teaspoons on greased baking sheet
Dip a dinner fork in flour then press down on the tops of the
     dough
Bake in pre-heated oven at 325° for approximately 10 minutes
Cool on rack or paper towels.

Notes:

Add coarsely chopped peanuts to batter
Add chocolate chips to batter
Get wild, add both

Biscotti

I love biscotti. Whenever I take a coffee or tea break these cookies make it special but you know how much they cost. And they are so easy to make. They're great for gifts, for freezing and of course for eating.

What you need:

1 cup of sugar
½ cup unsalted butter, melted
3 tablespoons brandy (Amaretto, Frangelica, rum or other liquor can be substitiuted)
1 teaspoon vanilla
1 teaspoon almond extract
1 cup coarsely chopped almonds (blanched)
3 eggs
3 cups flour
1 ½ teaspoons baking powder
1/4 teaspoon salt

How to assemble:

Preheat oven to 350°
Mix together the first five ingredients
Add nuts and eggs and mix well
Stir in flour mixed with baking powder and salt
Shape into a long loaf
Place on cookie sheet (sprayed with PAM)
Bake 20 to 30 minutes until loaf is slightly firm and cake like
Remove from oven and cool until loaf is comfortable to handle

Cut into ½ inch diagonal slices
Lay each slice on a cookie sheet, sliced side up
Return to oven and bake for 15 minutes more
Turn each slice over and bake another 15 minutes
Biscotti should look toasted on each side
Frost the biscotti with melted semisweet chocolate or canned frosting
    (optional)
Cool completely, then store in an air-tight jar

Notes:

Substitute 3/4 cup of chopped pecans and another of dried fruit (cranberries or cherries or apricots) then substitute appropriate liquor such as Cherry Herring or Apricot Brandy for the brandy.

Make up your own combination.

Coconut Delights

I found this on a soda cracker box but then I changed it as I usually do, to suit myself. If you love the soft, chewy, almond-flavored coconut macaroons, this is your cookie. Besides, they freeze wonderfully well. Let unexpected company drop by, iced tea or coffee and this cookie will impress them no end.

What you need:

2 ½ cups of coconut
1 cup coarsely chopped macadamia nuts
1 cup chocolate chips
20 saltine crackers (small squares) finely crushed
1 teaspoon almond extract
1 cup sweetened condensed milk
2 egg whites

How to assemble:

Heat oven to 350°
Beat egg whites until stiff
Mix almond extract into condensed milk,
Stir in coconut, nuts, chocolate chips and cracker crumbs
Fold in egg whites
Drop by teaspoons on a cookie sheet, lightly sprayed with PAM
Bake for approximately 12 minutes (cookies should be turning
    golden brown)

Notes:

Crescent Dinner Rolls

These were the dinner rolls we served every Thanksgiving when I was a kid. My mother mixed them up the night before and my sister and I prepared them on Thanksgiving morning after the turkey went in the oven. I used to make them for my Thanksgiving dinners but then Thanksgiving started getting so big I couldn't do everything and maintain my sanity. Just about that time my friend, Sherrill, started joining us and she brought her rolls. One year Sherrill had a problem with her wrist and couldn't make the rolls so I made these.

Several years later, after spending a Thanksgiving at my sister's place in Oregon instead of with me, she was surprised to have the same dinner rolls. She then confessed that for all those years she thought I must have bought the rolls that were so delicious. It wasn't until she saw my sister's that she realized I was telling the truth when I said it was an old family recipe.

You don't have to wait for Thanksgiving, they're easy enough for any nice dinner party.

What you need:

1 package dry yeast
1 tablespoon white sugar
1/4 cup warm water (not hot)
½ cup melted butter or margarine
3/4 cup milk
2 eggs
1/3 cup sugar
3/4 teaspoon salt
4 cups flour
1 cube softened butter or margarine

How to assemble:

Mix the dry yeast, the tablespoon of sugar and the warm water to
 activate the yeast

In a mixing bowl combine the melted butter, milk, beaten eggs,
 salt and 1/3 cup of sugar

Mix well

Add the yeast mixture and again mix well

Slowly add the flour until completely mixed, dough should stick
 together to form a big ball

Cover the dough in the bowl with plastic wrap and refrigerate over
 night

About 4 hours before baking remove dough from refrigerator

Cut dough into 4 equal parts

Knead one section slightly on a floured board

Roll out dough in a circle but turning over and around as you
 would a pie crust

When the circle is approximately 12" diameter spread it lightly
 with the softened butter or margarine

Cut each circle into 8 wedges

Roll each wedge from the outside to the tip and lay on a greased
 baking sheet with the tip side down

Form each roll in a slight crescent shape leaving a little space around
 it to allow for the dough to rise

Repeat this process until all the dough has been formed into
 rolls

Let rise in the kitchen until rolls are approximately double in size
 (3 hours)

Just before dinner bake the rolls at 350° for 10 to 15 minutes

Cool for five minutes before serving

Notes:

These make wonderful cinnamon roll if you add sugar and
cinnamon mixture on top of the melted butter and sprinkle with

nuts and/or raisins just before you roll up the wedges. After the rolls are removed from the oven, drizzle them with icing (canned or homemade) before serving.

Double-Chocolate Almond Biscotti

Yes, its another biscotti recipe. But I warned you I loved them and I've spent a fortune buying them. And none I've bought have been any tastier then the three recipes you'll find in this book. So relax with your coffee and tea and indulge yourself, they're reasonable to make and fun. And a dozen or so of these make a great hostess gift for a dinner invitation instead of the obligatory bottle of wine.

What you need:

2 cups flour
1/3 cup unsweetened cocoa powder
1 ½ teaspoons baking powder
½ teaspoon salt
1/4 lb. unsalted butter at room tempature
1 1/4 cups of sugar
2 eggs
1 teaspoon vanilla extract
½ teaspoon almond extract
1 cup blanched almonds, coarsely chopped (any nut could be substituted)
2/3 cup semisweet chocolate chips

How to assemble:

Heat oven to 325°
Combine flour, cocoa, baking powder and salt and set a side
Beat butter and sugar until light and fluffy
Add in eggs, vanilla and almond extracts and continue beating
Gradually beat in flour mixture

Stir in nuts and chocolate chips

Shape dough into two logs about 1 ½" wide by 15" long

Place logs about 3" apart on a baking sheet, which was sprayed with PAM

Bake until edges start to brown and top becomes firm, 50 to 55 minutes

Cool until they can be handled comfortably

Cut into ½" diagonal slices

Return to baking sheet, cut side down and bake 15 to 20 minutes on each side

Cool and store in air tight containers.

Notes:

These can be iced if you so desire, melt more semi-sweet chocolate and dip the cookies. Let cool before storing.

Early California Egg Bread

Years ago when my daughter was a baby, one of the ladies at work made this and brought a loaf to work to share. It was so good I decided I had to make it. I planned a whole Saturday around baking bread and still getting my chores done. I scheduled the kneading and rising times to fit between my daughter's naps and my chores. Then I invited some friends over for dinner to share the bread and admire my culinary skills.

Making bread is time consuming but it is a strangely satisfying task. The day went beautifully and the bread (2 loaves) came out of the oven smelling heavenly and looking like a picture in a magazine. But the bread was too delicious. Somehow the three of us managed to eat not only the dinner I served and the desert but both loaves of bread. And I had nothing but memories the next day. All that work and not even a slice for toast in the morning.

What you need:

1 package of dry yeast
2 cups lukewarm water
1 cup + 2 tablespoons of sugar
6 cups of sifted flour
½ cup butter
1 teaspoon salt
2 large eggs

How to assemble:

Dissolve yeast in 1/4 cup of warm water and 2 tablespoons of sugar to activate the yeast

After yeast mixture bubbles add remaining water and stir

Mix in 3 cups of flour and beat until smooth

Cover and let rise to double size (approximately 1 ½ hours in a warm room)

When dough has doubled punch down

In a separate bowl cream butter, remaining sugar, salt and eggs

Mix dough and egg mixture until thoroughly blended

Stir in last 3 cups of flour a little at a time (dough will be slightly sticky)

Turn dough out on floured board and knead for approximately 10-15 minutes

Put it back in an oiled bowl, cover it lightly with plastic wrap and let it rise again to double size (approximately 1 ½ hours in warm room)

When dough has doubled punch it down and cut it into 2 pieces

Let the pieces rest for about 10 minutes

Shape each piece into a loaf shape

Put each into a greased loaf pan and let rise once more (double in size)

Bake at 350° for 40-45 minutes

Let cool before slicing and serving

Notes:

English Scones

Dave loves scones and I enjoy them served at an English Tea with Clotted Cream and strawberry jam. But scones are really only a variation of the shortcake I make from the Bisquick's box recipe for strawberry shortcake. So why am I bothering to give you this recipe? It's because of the English relatives who wouldn't like to hear I use Bisquick. Actually, these aren't difficult, try them for fun.

What you need:

1 cup flour
½ teaspoon salt
3 tablespoons butter
1 egg beaten
2 tablespoons sugar
½ cup milk
2 tablespoons of currents, blueberries or dried cherries

How to assemble:

Mix flour and salt
Cut in cold butter
Mix in sugar and fruit
Stir in egg except for 1 tablespoon reserved for later
Add enough milk to make a soft dough (dough should form soft
    ball in bowl)
Turn out dough on floured board
Form into a patty about ½ inch thick

Cut in rounds, squares or triangles
Place on a greased baking sheet
Brush top with beaten egg
Bake in a preheated oven at 425° for approximately 10 minutes
Serve hot with butter and jam

Alternatives:

1 cup of Bisquick instead of the flour, salt and butter
These scones can be dropped by the spoon on the baking sheet
   intead of rolled and cut.

Notes:

Friendship Bread Starter

I almost didn't include this recipe and the one following because it can ruin lives! I'm not sure giving this to a person is an act of friendship. Surely the gift of the bread is but the starter carries obligations and responsibilities. It has and can become all consuming. My friend, Vanya, gave me some and the next thing I knew I made forty-five breads, one for each of my employees, all my neighbors and every relative I had living close to me. I had to keep track every day less my starter DIE. Finally, I stopped from sheer exhaustion, on the brink of financial ruin from buying more and more ingredients. When I confessed my perfidy, Vanya admitted her own guilt. She too had succumbed when her freezer reached capacity and all her friends refused to answer their doors when they saw her coming with her gift.

So the only reason I can justify giving you the Friendship Bread recipe is to include the recipe for the starter, which neither Vanya nor I had. Now you can actually throw away the starter and begin again when you want. You are no longer forced to comply with the schedule to keep the darn think alive. Kill it whenever you want, it's only sugar, flour and yeast. It is not alive, at least not as we know life. Trust me, you can start again.

So, why bother? Well the Friendship Bread is quite delicious. My husband became somewhat addicted to it. So someday, a few years in the future, I may bake it again. Or perhaps one of you will and I will gladly take some of it off your hands. The bread that is, not the starter.

What you need:

2 cups unbleached, all-purpose flour
2 cups warm water

1 package active dry yeast
Additional milk, flour, sugar as instructed

How to assemble:

Day 1:
Mix the above in gredients in a glass or ceramic bowl. Leave on kitchen counter uncovered. *Do not refrigerate.*

Days 2, 3 & 4:
Each day stir well with a wooden spoon (do not use a metal spoon)

Day 5: *Feed the Starter*
Add 1 cup milk, 1 cup flour and 1 cup sugar. Stir well. Leave on kitchen counter. *Do not refrigerate.*

Days 6, 7 & 8:
Each day stir well with a wooden spoon (do not use a metal spoon)

Day 9: *Feed the Starter*
Add 1 cup milk, 1 cup flour and 1 cup sugar. Stir well. Leave on kitchen counter. *Do not refrigerate.*

Days 10 & 11:
Each day stir well with a wooden spoon (do not use a metal spoon)

Day 12:
Divide starter into four containers. Use one container to bake 2 Friendship Breads. Store the other containers in the refrigerator or freezer for future use. Or give a container to a friend at the risk of jeopardizing the friendship.

Using refrigerated starter:

Every ten days it has to be fed or it dies. You can imagine your refrigerator after a couple of months. Better to freeze it or give it away. No wonder Vanya talked me into taking some, she was desperate.

In order to use frozen starter let it thaw and come to room temperature, then use it to cook.

Good luck!

Notes:

Vanya and Jerry Hilbert, friends since the 50's If you see her coming with a batch of starter don't answer the door.

Friendship Bread

This is a moist, heavy loaf cake (bread) somewhat similar to a sour cream coffee cake. After all the varieties I made I found our favorite to contain dried cherries and pecans but it's good with raisins and other nuts, too. This recipe will make two regular loaf pans of bread but I used copper molds to make pretty cakes. It cooks more evenly in a pan with a tube in the middle. Cooled and wrapped well they keep for months in the freezer and are a welcome gift.

Warning: Don't start this without reading the full disclosure under Friendship Bread Starter.

What you need:

1 cup Friendship Bread Starter (see recipe in this book)
1 cup vegetable oil
3 eggs
½ cup milk
1 teaspoon vanilla
2 cups flour
1 ½ teaspoons baking powder
1 cup sugar
2 teaspoons cinnamon
1 large box Instant Vanilla Pudding
½ teaspoon salt
½ teaspoon baking soda
1 cup chopped nuts
1 cup dried cherries (or other dried fruit)

How to assemble:

Heat oven to 350°
Spray two or three pans liberally with PAM
Put starter in large bowl
Add oil, eggs, milk and vanilla and mix well
In a separate bowl mix flour, baking powder, sugar, cinnamon,
    pudding, salt and baking soda
Slowly add dry ingredients to egg mixture, stirring well
Add fruit and nuts
Pour batter in pans (do not fill more than 2/3's full)
Sprinkle top of each bread with a mixture of cinnamon and sugar
    (optional)
Bake for approximately 1 hour (or until a toothpick inserted in the
    middle of the loaf comes out clean)
Cool, remove from pan and serve. Or wrap as a gift, or store in the
    freezer.

Notes:

Gert's Oatmeal Date Bars

Ken and Gert were long time friends of my parents. In fact Ken worked at the Bomber Plant in Ann Arbor with my dad and moved to California at the same time we did to go into business with my dad and some other men. While the business didn't last the friendship did. Connie and I took turns babysitting for their children during our high school years.

This was a recipe Gert gave my mom and she subsequently made these for the holidays each year. She would make them early hoping they would last to Christmas but they rarely did no matter whether or not she doubled or tripled the recipe.

What you need:

Crust:
1 3/4 cups oatmeal
1 ½ cups flour
1 cup brown sugar (packed)
1 teaspoon baking soda
½ teaspoon salt
3/4 cups butter

Filling:
3/4 cup of stoned dates, chopped
1 cup water
3/4 cup walnut or pecan pieces (optional)

How to assemble:

In a heavy sauce pan boil the fruit, sugar and water for the filling until the mixture becomes thick (approximately 30 minutes)

Remove from fire and add nuts

Set aside and let cool

Meanwhile, cream the butter and brown sugar together

In a separate bowl mix the oatmeal, flour, soda and salt together

Add the dry ingredients slowly to the butter/sugar mixture and mix thoroughly until it forms a ball

Divide the dough in half

Pack one half of the dough in the bottom of a 9 x 9 square cake pan so it forms a smooth bottom crust

Pour the cooled fruit mixture evenly over the crust

Sprinkle the remaining dough evenly over the pan

Press down dough forming a top crust

Bake in a pre-heated oven at 375° for about 40 minutes or until the top crust is golden brown

Remove from oven and cool

Cut into bars about 1" by 2" and serve.

Variations:

Your family doesn't like dates? No problem. These are wonderful with dried cherries, or apricots, or cranberries. Or all of them together.

Notes:

Grandma Janet's Oatmeal Cookies

Grandma Janet was Dave's mother and we all loved her dearly. She was bright, spunky and fun. She was born in 1898 and she could share her memories with us until she passed away at the age of 93. Until the last few years of her life she made these cookies every Christmas along with her sugar cookies. For some reason I didn't get a copy of this recipe and didn't make these cookies until my little sister, Teresa, reminded me. Teresa had written the recipe down on one of her visits and makes them all the time. The name Oatmeal is a misnomer. I always called them Lemon Cookies but the recipe proves they are oatmeal cookies. Teresa uses Almond Extract or Vanilla instead of the Lemon Extract so for a while we were both confused.

What you need:

1 ½ cups margarine or butter (3 cubes)
1 ½ cups granulated sugar
3 cups of flour
½ teaspoon of salt
2 eggs
1 cup oatmeal
1 ½ teaspoon of lemon extract (or almond or vanilla)

How to assemble:

Mix together margarine, sugar, flour and salt like a pie crust
Add eggs, oatmeal and flavoring and mix well
Roll teaspoons of dough into a ball and place on a cookie sheet
   sprayed with PAM

Flatten each ball with a bottom of a glass dipped in granulated
sugar
Place in a pre-heated oven at 350°
Bake for 8-12 minutes until cookies edges are golden brown
Remove cookie sheet and cool slightly before removing cookies to
rack or paper towel for complete cooling
Store in airtight container or freeze until serving

Notes:

Janet Cunningham Wigglesworth, Dave's mother,
the kids' grandmother and my good friend.

Grandma Janet's Sugar Cookies

When Grandma Janet was a young girl she made a mistake when she baked cookies for the family. The results were so pleasing she made these cookies ever since. When her eyesight began to fail her I took over the responsibility of making them every Christmas. But they're good any time of the year. I even won a local baking contest using this recipe.

What you need:

1 ½ cups *melted* margarine or butter (3 cubes)
2 cups of brown sugar (packed tightly in cup)
2 eggs
4 cups flour
1 teaspoon baking powder
1 cup of walnut or pecan pieces

How to assemble:

Mix melted margarine and sugar until smooth
Add eggs and continue to mix well
Add baking soda
Slowly add the flour, mixing well
Stir in the nuts
Divide the dough into fourths
Form each section of dough into a log
Wrap each log in plastic wrap or aluminum foil and store in
   refrigerator for at least three hours

How to bake:

Heat oven to 350°
Prepare two baking sheets by spraying with PAM
Remove one roll of dough at a time from the refrigerator
Using a very sharp knife cut very thin slices (I once used my electric
    slicer and it worked very well)
Arrange the slices on the cookie sheet at least 1 inch apart
Bake for 8-12 minutes until cookies are golden brown
Remove cookies from oven and cool slightly before removing from sheet.
Cool completely on paper towel or rack.

These cookies are very crispy and should be kept in an airtight
    container or freezer until serving time.

Notes:

This dough can be stored in the refrigerator for several weeks
or even frozen if you don't want to cook all of them at one time.

Granny's Banana Bread

This was one of my mother's favorites. She called it the Best Banana Bread and submitted it to several of her church and club community cookbooks. It's full of banana flavor and moist. If you want to sell your house, bake a loaf of this before the open house and leave a platter of it for people to taste. It makes the house smell heavenly and it should put them in a good mood.

What you need:

3 ripe bananas, mashed
1/3 cup cooking oil
½ cup milk
1 cup granulated sugar
1 egg
2 cups of all purpose flour
1 teaspoon salt
1 teaspoon baking powder
1 teaspoon baking soda
½ teaspoon ground cinnamon
1/4 teaspoon ground cloves
1/4 teaspoon ground nutmeg
Option:
2 cups blueberries (fresh or frozen, then thawed)
1 cup of nuts (I like pecans)

How to assemble:

Measure out flour, spices, salt, soda and baking powder and set aside
Beat banana, sugar, oil mild and egg together until smooth and blended

Slowly add dry ingredients to banana mixture and beat until batter
is smooth
Add nuts and blueberries if desired
Pour into 1 large bundt cake pan which has been sprayed with PAM
(you can use 2 loaf pans or a sheet cake pan)
Bake at 350° for approximately 45 minutes to 1 hour or until a
toothpick inserted in the middle comes out clean.
This bread freezes nicely

Hints:

This is best made with very ripe bananas and if you're like I
am you don't like to eat your bananas when brown spots appear on
the skin. So when your bananas reach this stage, peel them, put
them in a freezer bag, three to a bag and freeze them until you feel
like baking.

I always add blueberries to this recipe and I hear my sister,
Connie, does too. When blueberries are available in the stores,
Dave always buys several big boxes, picks through them to discard
stems and hard ones then dumps them in freezer bags (do not
wash them). They freeze like marbles and can be used frozen or
thawed throughout the year.

Notes:

*Margaret Kilmartin and Jo Coates visiting us
sometime in the 80's. Margaret and mom were dear
friends and the Kilmartins were part of our family
and shared all of the Coates' holidays.*

Johnnie Cake (Corn Bread)

This is a great addition to a meal of soup or chili. It came out of my grandmother's little brown notebook but since I've been making this all my life, I've put it in this section of the cookbook instead of her section. I just guess at the amount of the ingredients and somehow it always turns out great.

What you need:

lard or butter the size of an egg (4 tablespoons)
salt (1 teaspoon)
½ cup sugar
1 ½ cups milk
1 ½ cups each of cornmeal and flour
2 eggs
3 teaspoons baking powder

How to assemble:

Cream the butter, salt and sugar together
Add eggs, mixing well
Add milk
In a separate bowl add cornmeal, flour and baking powder together
Stir dry mixture into the other batter, beating well
Pour into a square, buttered cake pan (spray with PAM)
Bake at 350° for about 30 minutes or until a toothpick inserted in
the middle comes out clean.

Notes:

Don't be afraid to add something to the batter like chopped green chili's or corn with red peppers, or even grated cheese.

Lemon Bars

After Dave and I married we continued his family's tradition of having a big, sit down Sunday dinner. All the kids, Grandma Janet and any other relative or friend in the area would join us. Grandma Janet used to bring a pan of lemon bars and a bag of homemade chocolate chip cookies to each of the dinners. You can imagine how all the kids looked forward to her arrival. We never got tired of them and they never had to be thrown away.

What you need:

Crust:
1 cup flour
1/4 cup powdered sugar
½ butter or margarine

Filling:
2 eggs
2 tablespoons of flour
1 cup of sugar
1 tablespoon of grated lemon rind (the yellow part not the bitter white part)
2 tablespoons lemon juice
½ teaspoon baking powder
1 tablespoon powdered sugar (to sprinkle on top of baked bars)

How to assemble:

Heat over to 350°
Spray a 9" x 9" square cake pan with PAM

Mix the first three ingredients into a dough similar to pie crust and press evenly in the bottom of the baking pan

Bake for 15 minutes and then remove from oven

Mix remaining ingredients well and pour over the baked crust

Return pan to the oven and bake another 25 minutes

Remove from oven and cool completely

Sprinkle powdered sugar over the top and cut into bars and serve

Notes:

Macadamia Shortbread

These are as good as they sound. I've been making them for Christmas for the past fifteen years. It's an elegant and easy cookie and it happens to be Mitch's favorite.

What you need:

1 cup macadamia nuts (about 8 ozs.)

3 cups cake flour (the fine grind of this flour adds to the texture of the cookie)

3/4 cup confectioner's sugar (I used powdered sugar)

1 1/4 cups of butter or margarine (2 ½ cubes) at room temperature

1 cup of semisweet chocolate chips (1 6oz package will do)

How to assemble:

Heat oven to 325°

Use your Cuisinart on this one if you have it

Grind ½ cup of the macadamia nuts until it becomes a fine paste

Add the flour and sugar and mix with short bursts of power

Cut butter into small hunks and add, still using short bursts. The dough should resemble a pie crust dough and stick together in a ball

Spray a 13" x 9" baking pan with PAM

Pat dough evenly into the pan

Bake approximately 40 minutes or until dough is lightly browned

Remove the pan from the oven and immediately sprinkle the chocolate chips over the top

Meanwhile, coarsely chop the other ½ cup of nuts

Let the pan cool for five minutes then gently spread the softened
     chocolate chips over the top of the dough evenly
Sprinkle with chopped nuts and press them gently into the chocolate
Let cool another five minutes and then while still warm, cut into
     rectangles and then diagonally. Each piece will be a triangle.

Caution: Don't let the cookies get too cool before cutting or they
     will crumble and while they'll still taste good they are a mess
     to eat.

Notes:

Margaret's Bourbon Balls

I met Margaret when she worked for me at Wells Fargo and we've been friends ever since. Every year at Christmas she would make these and bring them to the office to share. I could tell when she had brought them in by the pitch of giggles that would begin a few hours into the day. These are very potent and should be consumed with extreme care. Children and pregnant women should not have access to them. But after all those warnings I do have to admit they're delicious. And if you like rum or another liquor, such as Frangelica or Amaretto, feel free to substitute that for the bourbon.

What you need:

6 oz. package of chocolate chips
3 tablespoons of light corn syrup
½ cup sugar
2 ½ cups crushed vanilla wafer cookie or graham cracker crumbs
½ cup nuts chopped finely
½ cup bourbon or other liquor of choice
Enough powdered sugar to coat each ball

How to assemble:

Melt chocolate chips in a double boiler
Add other ingredients
Stir until all ingredients are mixed thoroughly
Take a teaspoon of dough and roll it into a ball

Then roll the ball in powdered sugar (or shake them in a bag of
powdered sugar)
Store in an airtight container until served

Notes:

"Mrs. Field's" Cookies

This is another of those urban legends. Mrs. Field's Cookies were very popular and this was supposedly the recipe she used. However, Mrs. Field says its not. At any rate, Danielle likes them well enough to make them. I'm too lazy, more inclined to make my Oatmeal Chocolate Chip cookies. So we've worked out a deal. She makes the batter and I bake them. Everyone helps to eat them.

What you need:

1 cup butter (two cubes)
1 cup brown sugar (packed tightly)
1 cup granulated sugar
2 eggs
1 teaspoon vanilla
2 cups flour
2 ½ cups oatmeal
½ teaspoon salt
1 teaspoon baking powder
1 teaspoon baking soda
12 oz package semi-sweet chocolate chips
4 oz milk chocolate candy bar finely grated
1 ½ cups chopped nuts

How to assemble:

Cream together butter and both sugars
Add the eggs and the vanilla and mix well
Doing ½ the oatmeal at a time, use your blender to turn it into a
    fine powder and put it in a separate bowl

Add the flour, baking powder, soda and salt to the oatmeal and stir
it together

Add dry ingredients to egg mixture

When thoroughly mixed add the chocolate chips, the grated milk
chocolate and the nuts, and mix well

Drop by tablespoons on a greased cookie sheet about 1" apart

Bake at 350° degrees for 8-10 minutes

Cool for five minutes and remove to paper towel or rack to finish
cooling

Notes:

Nut Crunch Topping

This is a very versatile topping and can be used on cheesecakes, pies, cakes and even on ice cream. I also do this with pecan and walnut halves and keep them in the freezer to be added to my Blue Cheese, Pear salad (see that section of the book).

This recipe makes enough to sprinkle on the top of one pie or cake but you can hardly go wrong if you just double it so you have some to store in the freezer for another occasion.

What you need:

2 tablespoons butter or margarine
1/3 cup of packed brown sugar
3/4 cup of walnuts or pecans pieces

How to assemble:

Melt the butter and brown sugar in a small pan
Stir until bubbling
Pour the nuts into the pan and stir to coat nuts evenly
Cook until the nuts have absorbed the glaze
Spoon over the cake or pie (or on a cookie sheet to cool before storing)

Notes:

Oatmeal Chocolate Chip Cookies

I grew up with these cookies. For many years we didn't even know there were other kinds of chocolate chip cookies, like the one on the back of the chocolate chip package. My sister, Connie, and I would bake every Saturday and we would make a triple batch of these cookies. They were always gone by Monday evening. Now that I look back I don't think any of us ever had to ask for a cookie, if they were there we ate them when we wanted them. And frequently for breakfast a few cookies with a glass of milk for dunking couldn't be beat.

Some Saturdays for variety we'd make the chocolate chip triple batch and then make a double batch with coconut and peanuts. I get hungry just thinking about it.

What you need:

1 cup margarine or butter (2 cubes) at room temperature
1 cup brown sugar (packed)
1 cup granulated sugar
2 eggs
1 teaspoon vanilla
2 tablespoons of warm water
1 teaspoon of salt
1 teaspoon of baking soda
1 ½ cups flour
3 cups oatmeal
1 12 oz package of chocolate chips

How to assemble:

Heat oven to 350°
Spray two baking sheets with PAM
Cream together butter and sugars until smooth
Beat the eggs in a small bowl and add to butter mixture
Mix well
Put the water in a small bowl and add baking soda and salt to it.
　　Stir until the soda and salt are dissolved then add it to the
　　batter and mix in well
Slowly add the flour, mixing it well as you go
Add the oatmeal a cup at a time until the batter is completely mixed
Stir in chocolate chips and/or nuts
Drop by generous teaspoons to the baking sheet about 1" apart
Bake until golden brown (approximately 12-15 minutes)
Remove and let cool for five minutes before removing to rack or
　　paper towels to completely cool.
Store in airtight containers until eaten

Variations:

As I mentioned, growing up we frequently added coconut and peanuts to a batch instead of chocolate chips.

Sometimes I add peanuts or other nuts to the chocolate chips.

On special occasions I've added trail mix to this recipe for a wonderful cookie

Notes:

This is a double recipe because it's not worth making only one. You'll find you can eat half of them while you're baking them. These cookies do freeze very well if you want to limit how many are available to you. By the way these cookies are soft and warm right out of the oven but crisp up as they cool. Try dunking them in coffee or milk.

Recently I was in a hurry so I pressed the dough into a thin layer on the bottom of two large baking dishes and baked them both at the same time. I then cut them into bars and was very pleased with the results. And it took so little time I may never go back to baking individual cookies again.

Peanut Brittle

I started making this while I was still in high school and it became a family Christmas favorite. I got the recipe out of an old cookbook my mother had, which has since disappeared. When I moved away from home in 1964 my mother took over making this candy and became quite an expert. She used to go to a special store to get the raw peanuts and then cooked them in the candy. But I just used regular peanuts and followed this recipe. It's easy and tasty.

What you need:

2 cups granulated sugar
½ cup light corn syrup
½ cup water
3 tablespoons of butter or margarine
2 cups peanuts
½ teaspoon vanilla
1/8 teaspoon baking soda
1/8 teaspoon salt

How to assemble:

Assemble the butter, vanilla, baking soda and salt in a small
      container and set aside
Spread the peanuts evenly over a greased slab or baking sheet
Combine the sugar, corn syrup and water in a large cast iron skillet
      (if you don't have one use a heavy skillet)
Bring to a boil, stirring occasionally to thoroughly mix all ingredients
Let boil until mixture turns a golden brown, be careful it doesn't

get too dark and smell scorched. Note: it doesn't get light brown all over, just in spots and that's okay

When the candy has reached the desired golden brown (if using a thermometer it would be at the hard crack stage) remove the skillet from the heat and add in the butter mixture

Stir quickly as the candy will bubble and foam, turning from a transparent mixture to an opaque one

Pour the mixture over the greased slab of peanuts

When mixture has cooled enough to touch, butter your hands and pull out on the edges to stretch the candy out and make it thinner

When cool and brittle, use a knife handle to crack into pieces

Store in an air tight container until served.

Variations:

Use different nuts
Use coconut
Use it all

Notes:

Persimmon Cookies

A friend of mine had a large property that contained about a dozen persimmon trees. He went crazy when the fruit ripened and was always trying to give them away. I took them the first time because a basket of persimmons looked beautiful on the table or in the kitchen but then I began thinking I should do something with them. I started collecting recipes and experimenting so when Dave and I moved to a house in San Mateo, with its own persimmon tree, I was ready.

This cookie was Grandma Janet's favorite cookie. So after all those years of her supplying us with cookies I tried to keep persimmon pulp in the freezer so I could reciprocate during the year.

One day after Danielle moved out, she came by to "borrower" some marinara sauce for a dinner she was cooking for guests that night.

I gave her a container and explained that it looked different frozen but not to worry it would heat up fine. She called me later to ask what she could do with polenta and hot persimmon puree which I had given her in error.

As Grandma Janet would have said, "Make cookies." I hope her guests had a sense of humor.

What you need:

1 cup sugar
½ cup butter or margarine (1cube)
1 cup persimmon pulp
1 teaspoon baking soda
1 egg
1 cup chopped walnuts or pecans
1 cup raisins (remember to prepare the raisins by pouring boiling

water over them, letting them set for 10 minutes, then draining
    them and drying them before adding them to the recipe)
2 cups flour
½ teaspoon cinnamon
½ teaspoon cloves
½ teaspoon nutmeg
1/4 teaspoon salt

How to assemble:

Heat oven to 350°
Add the soda to the persimmon pulp and set aside
Cream butter and sugar together
Add the egg and continue mixing
The baking soda will cause the persimmon pulp to gell, don't
    worry, just add it to the mixture and stir in well
Add the spices and salt to the flour you've measured out then
    slowly add the flour to the batter, mixing well
Add the nuts and raisins
Drop by spoonfuls on a baking sheet sprayed with PAM
Leave enough room for the cookies to rise
Bake 12 to 15 minutes or until the cookies are evenly brown
Remove and cool on a rack

These are a soft spicy cookie, excellent warm with coffee or cold milk.
These keep well frozen for up to a year if stored in zip lock baggies.

Notes:

Pear or heart shaped persimmons are the ones I use for the
recipes in this book. They are very hard and opaque when they're
picked but as they ripen they become soft and translucent. Cut
them in half and spoon out the soft fruit. The pulp will keep in
the refrigerator for several weeks, don't worry if it turns brown on

top, it's still good. I usually freeze it, 1 or 2 cups per container for later. But be sure to mark your containers, that's how Danielle got it by mistake.

Pistachio Biscotti

By now you've noticed my devotion to biscotti. This is yet another recipe but I had to include it as it is different from the others. Pick the recipe you like best and then use a variety of flavoring or nuts. Or be like me and make them all.

What you need:

3/4 cup sugar
½ cup butter or margarine (1 cube) at room temperature
2 eggs
1 teaspoon vanilla
1 ½ cups flour
½ cup yellow corn flour (polenta)
1 ½ teaspoons baking powder
1/4 teaspoon salt
1 ½ cups shelled, unsalted, chopped pistachios (divide in two parts)

How to assemble:

Heat oven to 325°
Beat butter and sugar until fluffy
Add vanilla and beat again
In a separate bowl assemble flour, cornmeal, baking powder and salt
Slowly add the dry ingredients to the butter mixture until just blended
Mix in ½ of nuts
Divide the dough into two parts

Shape each part of dough into a loaf and place on a greased baking
    sheet
Cover the top of the loaves with the remaining nuts and press
    lightly into the dough
Bake 45 minutes
Cool for 5 minutes then cut each log into slices
Place cookies, cut side down, on the baking sheet and return them
    to the oven
Bake on each side 10-15 minutes or until cookies are golden brown

Cool, then store in airtight container until served.

Notes:

Potato Chip Cookies

Those of you who know me know I'm a potter and worked for years at the Foster City Pottery Studio. On Tuesday night a group of 8-10 people congregate to play in the mud and one of the ladies occasionally decides to feed us. She had dietary constraints so when she cooks she has to get rid of the results. We're happy to be of help. This is one of her, and our, favorites. Try it for your family, they'll never guess it contains potato chips.

What you need:

1 cup butter or margarine (2 cubes)
½ cup sugar
2 cups flour
½ cup of crumbs made from crushed potato chips
½ cup pecans or almonds
1 teaspoon almond extract

How to assemble:

Cream butter, sugar and almond extract until it is light and fluffy
Add flour and mix well
Add potato chip crumbs and nuts and mix well
Form dough into small balls and place on greased cookie sheet
Using a large drinking glass, spray the bottom with PAM then dip
    in granulated sugar and use to press down on the ball of cookie
    dough to make a flat cookie

Repeat until all cookies on the sheet are ready to bake
Bake at 350° for 10 minutes

Notes:

Pumpkin Bread

My friend, Maureen, was the eldest of twelve children. However, unlike my family where my sister and I did much of the cooking, she wasn't allowed in the kitchen. So when she moved into her own apartment she was enthralled with the idea of cooking. She worked and worked on this recipe but could never get it right. It was good around the edges but the middle was a gooey mess.

Finally, she brought the stuff to my house and we did it together. There was nothing wrong with the recipe, just her oven. I've been making it ever since. It's one of those breads where you can make two, bake them in a pretty copper mold and then freeze one for a later occasion.

What you need:

1 ½ cups granulated sugar
1 ½ cups brown sugar (packed)
1 cup vegetable oil
4 eggs
2/3 cup of cold water
1 large can of pumpkin (2 cups or 16 ozs.)
3 1/3 cups of flour
2 teaspoons baking soda
1 ½ teaspoons salt
1 teaspoon cinnamon
1 teaspoon nutmeg
1 teaspoon Allspice
1 teaspoon pumpkin pie spice

1 cup nuts

1 cup dried fruit (diced apricots, cherries, cranberries, raisins or whatever you perfer)

How to assemble:

Mix the sugar, oil, eggs, water and pumpkin together in a large bowl

In a separate bowl measure out the flour, add the salt, soda and all the spices

Slowly stir the flour mixture into the pumpkin mixture then beat well

Add the nuts and fruit

Pour into greased pans taking care not to fill the pans more than 2/3's full

Bake at 350° for about 1 ½ hours or until at toothpick inserted in the middle comes out clean

Notes:

Pumpkin Pecan Bread

Here's another recipe for pumpkin bread which has all the flavor but only a quarter of the fat as in the preceding recipe. Do a test kitchen comparison to decide which one is best for you.

What you need:

3 cups flour
2 teaspoons baking powder
1 1/4 teaspoon salt
1 teaspoon baking soda
1 teaspoon ground cinnamon
1/4 teaspoon ground allspice
2 eggs
1 16oz can of pumpkin
1 cup brown sugar, packed
½ cup maple syrup
1/4 vegetable oil
½ cup raisins
½ cup chopped pecans

How to assemble:

Measure out the flour in a bowl and add the other 5 dry ingredients listed first above
In another container beat the eggs
Add the pumpkin, brown sugar, syrup and vegetable oil all the while beating well
Slowly add the flour mixture to the pumpkin mixture, stirring it thoroughly

Add the fruit and nuts

Pour into well greased loaf pan or bundt pan or tube pan taking care not to fill the container more that 2/3's full

Bake in a preheated oven at 350°until done (approximately 1 1/4 hours or until a toothpick inserted in the middle comes out clean

Notes:

Sandies, a Shortbread Cookie

These are a great favorite at my house, especially with Dave. I always make them for Christmas and for any other day that provides me with an excuse to bake. There are many variations to the cookies and some call it the Mexican Wedding Cookie. Call it what you want, its easy and delicious.

What you need:

1 cup butter (2 cubes) at room temperature
1/3 cup of granulated sugar
2 teaspoons water
2 teaspoons vanilla
2 cups all purpose flour
1 cup chopped pecans
½ cup powdered sugar

How to assemble:

Cream butter and sugar
Mix in water and vanilla
Blend in the flour and nuts
Chill dough for at least 4 hours
Heat oven to 325°
Shape dough into balls (about 1 tablespoon per cookie)
Place balls on ungreased baking sheet about 1" apart
Bake for 20 minutes or until the cookie is slightly golden brown

Cool for 10 minutes and then roll in powdered sugar or shake in a
   bag containing the sugar

Notes:

Scottish Raisin Scones

I know I gave you a recipe for scones earlier in this book but these are more like cookies and can be eaten as such. When I worked at EurekaBank the ladies were always competing with their baked goodies. A few of them even had their mothers participating. Erika was a Swiss lady and sometimes her mother would make these for us. I don't think they should be called scones because that brings another image to mind. But it's her recipe so I guess she can call it whatever she wants.

What you need:

2 cups of all purpose flour
2 teaspoons baking powder
½ teaspoon baking soda
1 teaspoon nutmeg
1/4 teaspoon salt
½ cup (1 cube) cold butter
1 cup raisins, dried cranberries or other dried fruit of similar size
4 tablespoons of sugar
1 large egg, separated
3/4 cup buttermilk
additional sugar to sprinkle on top

How to assemble:

Set oven to 375°
Mix first five ingredients together in a large bowl
Cut butter into chunks and cut into dry ingredients using fingers
    or a pastry blender until mixture looks like fine granules

Add dried fruit and sugar, toss mixture to distribute evenly

Add egg yolk to buttermilk and mix well

Pour mixture over dry ingredients and mix with a fork until soft dough forms

Turn dough out on a lightly floured board and knead 10 to 12 times

Cut dough in half and form each half into a ball

Flatten on floured board and shape into a 6 inch circle

Cut each circle into 6 wedges but do not separate

Beat the egg white with a whisk until the white breaks up

Brush the top of the shaped dough with the egg white then sprinkle lightly with sugar

Using a pancake turner, carefully transfer each circle of dough to a cookie sheet sprayed with PAM

Bake 18 to 22 minutes until medium brown

Cool on wire rack for five minutes then break circles into wedges

Continue to cool until serving, cover loosely with a dish towel

Notes:

"Sees" Fudge

I have no idea as to whether or not this is the real recipe for See's Fudge but that's what everybody said when my mother first got it in the 1950's. It's certainly good enough to be the real thing. It was something my mother made every Christmas and I think my sisters still do. I stopped making it a while back because I'm not that fond of fudge and it makes so much I never know what to do with it. But it's easy. If you like chocolate, you'll love this. And it could be See's recipe.

What you need:

1 large can evaporated milk
4 ½ cups sugar
1 pint marshmallow cream
3 small packages of chocolate chips (18ozs in all)
½ cup of butter or margarine (1 cube)
2 cups of nut pieces
1 tablespoon vanilla

How to assemble:

Assemble the marshmallow cream, chocolate chips, butter, nuts and vanilla in a large mixing bowl
Mix the evaporated milk with the sugar in a heavy saucepan and bring to a boil
Boil for 9 minutes stirring constantly to avoid scorching the bottom of the pan
Pour the boiling mixture over the other ingredients and beat the mixture vigorously

Beat until mixture is creamy and smooth
Pour into buttered pans
Cool
Cut into squares and finishing cooling in the refrigerator
When it is set (hard) its ready to serve
Keep refrigerated

Notes:

Sesame Delights

I know I mentioned working at EurekaBank before but it was significant part of my life so bear with me bringing it up again. Every year we would have three or four giant pot lucks. The whole fifth floor would participate and everyone developed favorites that they would insist that certain people supply. One of the ladies brought these once and then for ever more. If she signed up for something else people would hound her with requests for these. It was easier for her just to bring them. Try them yourself and see how good they are.

What you need:

2 cups sifted flour
1/4 teaspoon salt
½ teaspoon baking soda
1 cup butter or margarine (2 cubes)
1 cup sugar
1 egg
1 teaspoon vanilla
1/8 cup sesame seeds (2 tablespoons)
3/4 cup sugar frosted flakes crushed (this takes about 2 1/4 cups before crushing)

How to assemble:

Mix flour, salt, soda and ½ cup of cereal crumbs
In a separate bowl cream butter and sugar until light and fluffy
Add egg and vanilla to butter/sugar mixture and mix well
Add dry ingredients and mix well

Using a shallow dish combine the last 1/4 cup of cereal crumbs and the sesame seeds

Form cookie dough into 1" balls then roll each ball in the crumb/ seed mixture

Place each cookie on an ungreased cookie sheet about 1 ½" apart

Bake in a pre-heated oven at 375° for 10-12 minutes or until the cookie is lightly brown

Remove to rack or paper towel to cool

Store in an airtight container until served

Makes about 4 dozen cookies

Notes:

Sherrill's Yeast Rolls

A few years after I moved to San Francisco I couldn't take time off work to go home for Thanksgiving. My ex-roommate, Sherrill, was living in Watsonville and was given a turkey by her boss. So we decided to cook our own dinner and we invited several of our friends, who had nowhere to go for the holiday.

Sherrill arrived the night before with a monster turkey. Her reasoning was that as it was free she should get the biggest available and this one was more than 30 pounds. It barely fit in the refrigerator. We spent the evening preparing things for the next day and just before going to bed she mixed up a batch of her Grandmother's yeast rolls. I watched her add a hand full of this and pinch of that, awed by her confidence in the outcome despite her disdain of a recipe. Finally, the dough was ready, covered and tucked into the last available spot in my apartment-sized refrigerator.

I stumbled out of bed at six a.m. to wrestle that turkey into the oven and opened the refrigerator. The big pasty blob reached out to grab me, stretching grotesquely from the turkey, around various bottles and jars to containers stored in the door shelves. I staggered back, incoherently calling for help, crashing into Sherrill, who had leaped from bed at my first scream. Now it is funny. Then it wasn't.

The dough had risen, of course, and in that confined space it had crept into every inch of space it could find. And Sherrill reluctantly admitted she might have used a tad too much yeast. When I opened the refrigerator door it was just trying to escape.

And of course, she had made enough for an army so even with what remained permanently affixed to the bottles and jars and with what we threw away, we still had plenty of dough for everyone to enjoy her light, fluffy delicious rolls.

So during the past few years when Sherrill and her son Kurt,

*moved back to our area and started joining our Thanksgiving group,
she had to bring the yeast rolls. Now I don't have to worry about
that dough coming after me but I'll never forget it.*

What you need:

2 cups scalded milk
2 tablespoons sugar
1 teaspoon salt
1 tablespoon shortening (Crisco or butter)
1 package dry yeast
1/4 cup warm water
6 cups of sifted all purpose flour

How to assemble:

Mix sugar, salt and shortening in scalded milk and set aside to cool
    to lukewarm
Mix yeast and warm water until thoroughly dissolved
Combine the yeast mix to the milk mix
Add 3 cups of the flour and beat well
Add the remaining 3 cups of flour slowly, working the flour into
    the dough until the dough forms a ball and pulls away from
    the sides of the bowl
Turn the dough out on a floured board and shape it into a smooth ball
Cover the ball with a warm, damp cloth and let rest for 15 minutes
Knead dough for 10 minutes on a floured board
Reshape in ball and put into an oiled bowl more that twice its size
Cover with plastic wrap or a damp cloth and let rise until its twice
    its size.
Note: You can refrigerate over night at this point
While dough is still in the bowl, punch a hole in the middle of the
    dough with your fist and work the hole bigger and bigger in
    the bowl.

Cover the dough again and let rest for 30 minutes

Turn out on floured board and pinch off pieces about ½ size of the
   roll you want and form the dough into a ball.
Place each ball on a large baking sheet about ½ inch apart.
Let the pan of rolls rise for about an hour in a warm place, they
   should double in size
Bake in a pre-heated oven at 400° for 30-40 minutes
Remove from the oven and brush tops lightly with melted butter
Serve warm

Makes about 2 dozen rolls

Notes:

   When dough is shaped into rolls and rising you can add variety
by brushing the top with slightly beaten egg white and sprinkling
with sesame or poppy seeds or toasted garlic or Parmesan cheese,
or several of these.

*A Thanksgiving at our house with grandchildren Nicole
and Amy, Kurt and his mother, my friend Sherrill*

Shortbread Jam Tarts

Feel like baking? Want to make something fun but simple? Try this one. You can use a variety of cookie cutters and jams to get different looks and tastes but the cookie is very easy.

What you need:

8 oz. cream cheese, room temperature
8 oz butter or margarine (1 cup or 2 cubes), room temperature
2 cups flour
jam or preserves at needed

How to assemble:

Cream butter and cream cheese together
Slowly blend in flour until stiff dough ball is formed
On a floured board roll out dough to approximately 1/4" thick
Cut out the cookies with cookie cutters and lay them on a greased
    baking sheet
Depress center of each cookie with a spoon and fill the depression
    with jam or preserves
Bake in a pre-heated oven at 300° for 30 minutes or until the
    cookies turn slightly brown
Remove to racks or paper towel to cool

Notes:

Sour Cream Coffee Cake

Shortly after Diane married our son, Miles, she started to spoil us by bringing this treat to Christmas morning gatherings. This is a recipe her grandmother used so she had warm memories of it and she wanted to share it with her new family. We appreciated both the thought and the cake. During the past several years she has succumbed to the pressures of getting everything done for her immediate family and so has replaced this cake with store bought goodies but the sentiment is there and one of these days when her kids hit college age and her life is less hectic I'm sure we'll see this cake again.

What you need:

Cake:
1 ½ cups sugar
3/4 cup butter or margarine (1 ½ cubes) softened
3 eggs
1 ½ teaspoons vanilla
3 cups flour
1 ½ teaspoons baking powder
1 ½ teaspoons baking soda
3/4 teaspoon salt
1 ½ cups sour cream

Filling:
1 cup brown sugar, packed
½ cup finely chopped nuts
2 teaspoons ground cinnamon

How to assemble:

Cake:

Beat together butter, sugar, eggs and vanilla in a large mixing bowl

In a separate bowl mix flour, baking powder, baking soda and salt together

Alternatively add flour and sour cream to butter mixture until batter is mixed well

Pour 1/3 of the batter in a bundt pan which has been liberally sprayed with PAM

Mix the filling ingredients together

Sprinkle 1/3 of filling over batter in Bundt pan

Add another 1/3 of the batter in the pan evenly

Sprinkle another 1/3 of filling over the batter

Add the last of the batter and sprinkle the last of the filling on top

Bake in a pre-heated oven at 350° for approximately 1 hour or until a toothpick inserted in the middle of the cake comes out clean

Remove from oven and cool slightly

Invert on serving plate and remove pan, sprinkle powdered sugar on top before serving.

Notes:

Spicy Pineapple-Zucchini Bread

If you've ever grown zucchini or know any one who grows it, you'll understand the adage, if you want to plant zucchini just plant a quarter of a seed. Every summer offers of free zucchini are plentiful but how much can you eat? What can you do with them? Well here's a recipe that makes zucchini delicious and can be frozen for later in the year when you have forgotten your zucchini overload. And if you don't want anyone to know you used zucchini just peel the green skin off before grating them.

What you need:

3 eggs
1 cup vegetable oil
2 cups sugar
2 teaspoons vanilla
2 cups coarsely grated zucchini
1 can (8 1/4 oz) crushed pineapple, well drained
3 cups flour
2 teaspoons baking soda
1 teaspoon salt
½ teaspoon baking powder
1 ½ teaspoon cinnamon
3/4 teaspoon nutmeg
1 cup finely chopped nuts
1 cup raisins or dried cranberries

How to assemble:

Beat together eggs, oil, vanilla and sugar until thick and foamy

With a spoon stir in zucchini and pineapple
In a separate bowl combine flour, soda, salt, baking powder and spices
Stir the flour mixture gently into the batter, mixing well
Add the nuts and fruit
Pour into greased loaf pans or fluted pans
Bake in pre-heated oven at 350° for one hour or until a toothpick
    inserted in the cake comes out clean
Remove from oven and cool for 5 minutes
Invert on serving plate

These can be wrapped well and frozen at this point

Notes:

Sugared Peanuts

This was one of my mother's favorites. She had a special place she could buy raw peanuts and she liked to have these on hand to nibble on or serve to guests. I believe she liked to make them because they kept better than peanut brittle but still had the good peanut taste.

What you need:

3 cups large, raw, shelled peanuts
3/4 cups water
1 ½ cups sugar
dash of salt

How to assemble:

In a heavy sauce pan combine peanuts, water and sugar
Bing to boil over a medium heat
Boil until mixture crystalizes (about 10 minutes)
Remove from heat and spread on a greased baking sheet
Sprinkle with a little salt
Bake in oven pre-heated to 300° for 15 minutes
Stir peanuts, turning them over
Bake for another 15 minutes
Cool and store in an air tight container

Notes:

Teresa's Gingersnaps

Teresa may be my baby sister but she's still taught me a few cooking tricks over the years. This is a cookie she's made for a long time and when she had time she has even sent me some for Christmas. But when you make them yourself you get the bonus of a good smelling house on top of having the delicious cookies.

What you need:

2 cups flour
2 teaspoons baking soda
1 teaspoon cloves
1 1/4 teaspoon cinnamon
1 teaspoon ginger
1/4 teaspoon salt
1 cup sugar
1 egg
3/4 cup butter or margarine (1 ½ cubes) at room temperature
1/4 cup dark molasses

How to assemble:

Heat oven to 350°
Cream butter and eggs until light and fluffy
Add egg and molasses and beat
In a separate bowl measure out flour and the rest of the dry
    ingredients
Add dry mixture slowly to egg mixture, mixing well

Scoop up by tablespoons and roll into balls about 1" in diameter
Roll each ball of dough in a plate of granulated sugar before placing
    on a greased cookie sheet about 11/2" apart
Bake for approximately 15 minutes
Cool slightly before removing from cookie sheet

Notes:

Tortillas

Making tortillas is a family affair at our house. We only make them when we have black beans and pork but there is no law that states we can't do them whenever we want to. Our family has a tortilla press but two boards or flat bottomed plates could be used. Usually we have one person rolling the balls of dough, one person cutting the waxed paper squares, one person pressing the dough between two pieces of waxed paper on the tortilla press and one person cooking the tortillas. We all eat them.

What you need:

Equal amount of Masa Harina and white flour (check the packages for recommended amounts to use)
Water to make dough

How to assemble:

Mix the Masa Harina and flour with small amounts of water until dough forms a large ball
Form little balls of dough, about 1" in diameter
Note: if dough is too sticky add more flour and Masa Harina
Place ball between two sheets of waxed paper or in a sandwich bag and press flat with tortilla press or two boards
Peel the tortilla from the paper and place on a hot grill, do not use any oil
Cook each side about 5 minutes

Place tortilla in a warmer (we use a hollowed out gourd) until all are cooked and you're ready to serve

Notes:

Zucchini Bread

I debated putting this in because Dave and I can hardly look at a zucchini. But maybe in twenty or thirty years we will have forgotten that last huge crop we grew and might be willing to try it again. Or maybe you like zucchini.

What you need:

3 eggs
1 cup vegetable oil
1 cup white sugar
1 cup brown sugar, packed
2 cups grated zucchini
3 teaspoons vanilla
1 teaspoon salt
1 teaspoon baking soda
3 teaspoons cinnamon
1/4 teaspoon baking powder
3 ½ cups flour
1 cup chopped nuts (optional)

How to assemble:

Beat together the eggs, oil, vanilla and sugar until thick and foamy
In a separate bowl assemble all the dry ingredients
Slowly mix the dry ingredients into the batter
Add the nuts
Pour into two greased loaf pans or decorative flute pans
Bake in a pre-heated oven 325° for 60-70 minutes or until a
    toothpick inserted in the cake comes out clean

Cool for five minutes before inverting on a serving plate
Serve or wrap and store in the freezer

Notes:

Miles wife, Diane, who has graciously
taken over the Thanksgiving Holiday dinner.
She "does it by the book."

Munchies
and Noshes

A family dinner with Danielle, Janet, Miles and Diane

CONTENTS

Cheese Puffs

This delectable tasty is a real treat and served hot out of the oven they will be appreciated by all. What's even better is that these can be made up to 10 days before serving and stored in airtight freezer bags to be warmed and served with no fuss or bother on the appointed day. Try them.

What you need:

3/4 cup + 2 tablespoons flour
½ teaspoon salt
6 tablespoons unsalted butter cut into cubes
3/4 cup water
4 large eggs
4 ounces Gruyere cheese, coarsely grated

How to Assemble:

Preheat oven to 400° and set top rack at lower third of oven
Sift flour and set it aside
Combine salt, butter and water in a 1 ½ quart saucepan
Over medium heat bring mixture to rolling boil.
Immediately remove from fire and stir well
Add the flour all at once, stirring vigorously with a wooden spoon
until a stiff paste comes together in a ball
Return to medium heat, stirring quickly for about 10 seconds to
eliminate extra moisture
The paste should be smooth, thick and glossy
Put paste in large mixing bowl and cool for about 10 minutes

Using an electric mixer add the eggs and cheese slowly until completely incorporated into the dough

Spray a baking sheet(s) with PAM

Using teaspoons drop dough in 1 inch balls on cookie sheet leaving ½ inch between each one

Dip a pastry brush into a small amount of water and brush the tops of the puffs, this will smooth the dough

Bake 20 to 25 minutes until golden brown

Remove sheet to cooling rack and put next sheet in the oven to bake

Cool about 10 minutes and serve

Alternate:

Substitute Cheddar or Swiss cheese for a different flavor

Add ½ pound of cooked crisp, drained and crumbled bacon

Add ½ cup of finely chopped chives, either fresh or the equivalent freeze dried

Add ½ cup of finely chopped ham

Add herbs of your choice

If you are making ahead:

Cool completely

Pack loosely in zip lock freezer bags and freeze

Before serving place on cookie sheet frozen

Bake for about 8 minutes at 325°

Serve immediately

Notes:

Cheesy Garlic Bread

This makes a great hors d'oeuvre. If you serve it with dinner you may find everyone eating the bread instead of the dinner. This is very similar if not identical to the popular bread served at the Fish Market restaurants.

What you need:

1 can artichoke hearts packed in water
1 cup mayonnaise (I always use Hellman's or Best Foods)
1 cup grated Parmesan, Romano or Asiago cheese
1 teaspoon of garlic granules or 4 cloves fresh, crushed and chopped
1 loaf of sour dough or french bread

How to assemble:

Drain artichokes and chop fine
Add mayonnaise, cheese and garlic
Mix well
Chill for 1 hour to blend flavors
Slice bread in half horizontally
Spread each half liberally with mixture
Slice into serving size pieces but not all the way through the bread
Lay on ungreased baking sheet
Bake in a pre-heated oven at 350° for about 20 minutes or until
    the top in brown and bubbling
Remove from oven and serve hot

Notes:

Clam Garlic Dip

I don't know how I lived without my Cuisinart. We've made this dip for all the holidays since I was about ten and somehow I was always the one to make it. And it wasn't easy to mix the cream cheese and clams to the right consistency but now with modern conveniences it's a breeze. I especially like this with Fritos.

What you need:

1 can minced or chopped clams (6 ½ oz)
8 oz cream cheese cut into squares at room temperature
1 teaspoon granulated garlic or 2 fresh cloves smashed and chopped
1 tablespoon Worchestershire Sauce

How to assemble:

Drain clams but reserve liquid
Place all ingredients but clams and clam juice in the Cuisinart and
    process with short bursts of power
Add a little clam juice at a time until you reach the right consistency
Remove dip from Cuisinart and stir in clams
Chill thoroughly to set flavors
Remember, when you take this from the refrigerator it will be
    hard, and thicker than when its at serving temperature so
    remove it a hour before serving
Serve with chips, cracker or celery sticks

Notes:

Crustless Quiche (Frittata)

This dish is a great finger food, suitable for appetizers. I saw this on the Frugal Gourmet on day and wrote down my version of it. I made it for the get together at Grandma Janet's apartment after Diane and Miles' wedding. It worked great. I made it ahead and then warmed it just before serving. I use it when I do a holiday buffet as it makes a good addition to the table and is very popular.

What you need:

10 eggs beaten
½ cup flour
1 teaspoon baking powder
1/4 teaspoon salt
1 lb cottage cheese
1 lb shredded cheese (approximately 3 cups shredded) any kind or mix
1 cup sliced mushrooms
1 ½ cup chopped fresh spinach (packed tight)
½ cup chopped green onions

How to assemble:

In a large bowl mix ingredients together in same order as listed
    above
Pour into greased large baking pan (a lasagne pan would do)
Bake in a pre-heated oven at 400° for 15 minutes
Lower the oven temperature to 350° and bake for 30 minutes or
    until a knife blade inserted in the middle comes out clean
Cut into cubes and serve hot, room temperature or even cold
This can be frozen

Notes:

Add ham, cooked bacon, crab, shrimp, broccoli or other things instead of the mushrooms and spinach for variety.

Diane's Cheese Spread

Diane has been bringing this to special dinners and especially at Thanksgiving since she joined the family. It is a favorite. No matter how many times I say "Save your appetite for dinner" this is still demolished. She serves it in a hollowed out flat loaf of sour dough bread, surrounded by slices of beef stick and more slices of sour dough baguette and it just disappears.

What you need:

1 glass jar of Kraft Old English Cheese Spread
8 oz cream cheese
8 oz container of Westpride Smoked Hickory Spread
1 bottle of beer

How to assemble:

Combine cheeses in a mixing bowl
Slowly beat in 1/4 to ½ cup of beer
Add more beer as necessary to reach a nice spreading consistency
Put in hollowed out bread or in a dish and serve.

Notes:

If you have a Cuisinart its perfect for this recipe.
And of course you may as well drink the rest of the beer while you're making the spread.

Gloria's Crab Dip

Gloria worked with me at EurekaBank. She was a lady of many talents, painting, photography, almost any kind of art, and she loved to cook. Since she lived with her mother and they had limited appetites we all benefitted from her forays in the kitchen. This was a special favorite that she would share with us when the mood struck. Try it the next time you want to serve an hors d'oeuvre.

What you need:

1 can Cream of Mushroom soup
8 oz cream cheese cut into squares
1 package unflavored gelatin
½ cup chopped green onions
1 cup chopped celery
3/4 cup mayonnaise
8 oz cooked crab

How to assemble:

In a sauce pan heat the soup and cream cheese until hot and
    thoroughly blended (do not add water to the soup)
Remove mixture from the heat and stir in the gelatin
When this mixture has cooled, stir in the remaining ingredients
Pour this in a pretty serving bowl or a decorative mold
Chill until firm

Turn out on a plate and serve surrounded by crackers and cheese spreaders (Ritz crackers are especially tasty with this)

Notes:

Hot Chili Cheese Dip

Feel like a nibbley? Try this one on a cold and rainy evening. It's easy, tasty and not too disastrous for the diet.

What you need:

15 oz can of chili without beans (I'm particularly found of Hormel's
    Turkey Chili)
8 oz cream cheese, cut into squares
Tortilla Chips or Fritos Scoops

How to assemble:

In a sauce pan heat the chili and cream cheese until hot and
    thoroughly blended
Remove mixture from the heat and serve with chips

If you like picante (spicy hot) add a little cayenne pepper or a
    couple of drops of Tabasco Sauce and stir well.

Notes:

Kahlua

My mom got this recipe shortly before I moved to San Francisco. Kahlua and Black Russians were very popular drinks then and very expensive. I was extremely poor for many years and so I made this a lot. I gave it away for gifts, I served it with coffee, with milk, with vodka and at a huge Christmas party my roommates and I gave one year. Helen Gurley Brown had a recipe for ice cream drinks using Kahlua in her book, Sex and the Single Girl, *which was my bible in those days.*

Those were the days. I had no liquor but I always had jug wine and Kahlua. And the cheap jug wine provided me the vessels to make the Kuhlua in. Actually, I think this recipe makes a more tasty drink then the real stuff. Try it and see what you think.

What you need:

4 cups granulated sugar
2 oz instant coffee or instant expresso
2 cups boiling water
1 pint brandy (the higher the alcohol content the better, and
    cheaper is better)
1 whole vanilla bean

How to assemble:

Pour the boiling water over the sugar and instant coffee
Stir until completely dissolved
Slit the vanilla bean length wise
Scape out the gritty seeds from the inside and put seeds and outside
    of the bean in the coffee mix

Pour in the brandy and mix lightly

Pour the entire mixture into a large bottle

Seal and store in dark cool place about 1 month

Every week shake the bottle to allow the flavors to mix and mature

Anytime after the month is up you can take out Kahlua for serving but remember to pour it through a strainer and return any residue from the strainer to the bottle.

Keep the unused portion in the bottle with the vanilla bean and continue to shake occasionally, it will only get better.

Serving Suggestions:

Serve as a topping for ice cream

Mix one portion of Kahlua to 2 portions of vodka and serve over ice for a Black Russian

Mix one portion of Kahlua, 1 portion of vodka and one portion of heavy cream with ice in a blender for a White Russian

Serve one shot in a cup of coffee with a squirt of whipping cream on top for a Russian Coffee

Notes:

Shrimp Butter

My mother loved this one. She got it from one of her friends and found that she could make it, freeze part of it and have it when she was hungry for shrimp taste. Of course, she did this later in life when she had a blender and a freezer available. But she liked to cook and one of the frustrations as you get older is that there is no one to cook for. This worked for her and was very good.

What you need:

3/4 cup butter or margarine (1 ½ cubes)
8 oz cream cheese cut into squares
4 tablespoons of mayonnaise
1 tablespoon freshly grated onion
2 tablespoons of fresh lemon juice
12 oz fresh cooked shrimp, patted dry to remove excess moisture

How to assemble:

Place all ingredients in a Cuisinart or a blender and blend to butter
    consistency
Chill thoroughly before serving
Service with crackers and celery sticks

Makes 3 cups and can be frozen for future use

Notes:

Spinach Dip

You can get a recipe for this dip on the back of a Knorr Vegetable Soup box but my kids think this is better. Don't do what I did once and get the wrong kind of dried vegetable soup. I bought one that had pasta in it and people kept saying "what's this funny lumpy thing in the dip?" It tasted fine but it was a bit lacking in presentation.

What you need:

1 pint sour cream
2 cups fresh spinach leaves, washed, dried and packed tight
1/4 teaspoon garlic granules
1 package Knorr Vegetable Soup mix
8 oz can of water chestnuts

How to assemble:

Chop spinach leaves
Chop water chestnuts
Add to other ingredients and mix well
Refrigerate for 2 hours to meld flavors

Serve with chips, crackers and raw vegetables

Notes:

Because you're using fresh spinach don't be alarmed if it makes your dip light green. It will taste wonderful.

Turkey Puffs

This was originally Turtle Puffs but its hard to get turtle so I turned it into turkey but it could also be crab, chicken, ham, tuna or whatever your imagination comes up with.

When Dad went back to Michigan for a family reunion around 1970 he suffered a massive heart attack and all of us kids (except Teresa, who was only a child) flew to Michigan to be with him and Mom. Fortunately, he did recover. Connie and Gib returned home immediately but Cliff, Nick, his wife, Mary, and I stayed for a few days. The relatives wanted to entertain us and at the same time cut some slack for Winnie and Bernie, who were trying to cope with a house full of unexpected company. So they sent us up North. Aunt Kate and Uncle Phil had a place on a lake, as did Aunt Dorrie and Uncle Bill and their younger kids. Our cousins, Gary Watson and Marilyn and her husband John lived near there too. While we were visiting one of the neighbors gave a party and we all went. It was a chance to meet the locals and they made us very welcome. People in the north ate off the land if the opportunity lent itself. That meant fish, frogs, turtles, various game birds and deer, regardless of season.

The hostess served us these Turtle Puffs. We didn't ask if the turtle was in season.

I don't have turtle and don't even remember ever seeing it sold in our markets so I just substitute turkey but almost any filling will do.

What you need:

Puffs:
3/4 cup + 2 tablespoons flour
½ teaspoon salt
6 tablespoons unsalted butter cut into cubes
3/4 cup water
4 eggs

Turkey Salad:
3-4 cups cooked, chopped turkey (or crab, or ham, or whatever)
3 stalks celery, finely chopped
4 green onions, finely chopped
1/4 teaspoon garlic granules
salt and pepper to taste
½ cup chopped pecans
1 cup mayonnaise

How to assemble:

Puffs:
Preheat oven to 400° and set the top rack at the lower third of
    oven
Sift flour and set it aside
Combine salt, butter and water in a 1 ½ quart saucepan
Over medium heat bring mixture to rolling boil
Immediately remove from heat and stir well
Add the flour all at once, stirring vigorously with a wooden spoon
    until a stiff paste comes together in a ball
Return to medium heat, stirring quickly for about 10 seconds to
    eliminate extra moisture
The paste should be smooth, thick and glossy
Put past in large mixing bowl and cool for about 10 minutes
Using an electric mixer, add the eggs slowly until completely
    incorporated in the dough (note: if you're using jumbo eggs
    only use three to keep the dough from becoming too wet)

Spray a baking sheet with PAM

Using teaspoons drop dough in 1" balls on cookie sheet leaving ½ inch between them

Dip a pastry brush into a small amount of water and brush the tops of the puffs, this will smooth the dough

Bake 20 to 25 minutes, until golden brown

Remove to a rack to cool

After cooled slice the top off each puff

Cover them with a clean towel until ready to fill and serve

Turkey Salad Filling:

Mix all ingredients together with the mayonnaise

Taste for right amount of salt, pepper and mayonnaise and adjust if necessary.

Chill until ready to fill puffs

Serving Instructions:

One half hour before serving fill puffs

Using a teaspoon fill puff with turkey salad and set top in place

Try not to fill more than you will use in an hour as the filling will make the puffs soggy after a while.

If all the puffs aren't used, seal them in a freezer bag for another day

If using frozen puffs, take directly from the freezer and place on a baking sheet in an oven set at 325°for 8 minutes before filling

Notes:

These can be used as a dessert by filling with whipped cream, ice cream or pudding.

Gib and Linda, both family and friends, are known for the meals they put together.

Soups and Salads

Carving the turkey. Dave and Miles at work.

CONTENTS

Albondigas

My mother made this soup frequently when Teresa was growing up. I know because I use to go down to Southern California about once a month on business and of course stayed with them. I had it many times. Who knows where she got the recipe. She always liked Mexican food which was unusual for someone from a farm in rural Michigan. She told us when she was a little girl they had neighbors who had health problems and spent the winters in Arizona. The neighbors used to bring cases of canned chili back with them and shared it with all their neighbors. So mom developed a taste for Mexican food which lasted all her life. This recipe has the flavor of Mexico but is easy and economical which was just how my mother liked to cook.

What you need:

1 package Lipton Onion Soup mix
4 cups water
1 large can stewed tomatoes
2 tablespoons cumin
1 teaspoon garlic granules
2 teaspoons salt
1 lb ground beef
1 cup uncooked white rice
1 egg
1 small package frozen corn
1 small package frozen mixed vegetables
1 large can refried beans

How to assemble:

In a large heavy soup pot mix the water, onion soup mix, tomatoes,
    cummin, 1 teaspoon salt and garlic
Bring to a boil
Meanwhile in a separate bowl mix ground beef, rice, remaining
    salt and egg together
Form mixture into small meatballs about 1-1 ½ inches in diameter
Drop meatballs into boiling soup and cook about 30 minutes
Add frozen vegetables and refried beans
Simmer about 30 minutes, stirring it once or twice to mix beans
    into the soup
Serve

Notes:

Boston Clam Chowder

We love soup, especially on a winter day when you want to stay in and have the house filled with good smells. This is not the thick bland soup you're served in most restaurants. This tastes great and its easy.

What you need:

2 cans (6 ½ oz each) of minced or chopped clams
1 tablespoon butter
2 tablespoons dried, minced onions
1 teaspoon of garlic granules
½ teaspoon salt pepper to taste
2 large potatoes, peeled and diced
2 cups half and half (or two cups of no fat milk with 2 teaspoons of
   cornstarch dissolve in it)

How to assemble:

Drain the clams reserving the liquid and clam meat separately
In a heavy soup pot saute the dried onion in butter until the onion
   starts to turn light brown
Add clam juice, diced potatoes, garlic and salt
Cover pot and simmer until the potatoes are tender
Add half and half or milk and slowly bring to a boil (if you're using
   milk with cornstarch the soup has to come to a boil to thicken,
   if you're using half and half you just need to heat it thoroughly
Add the clams and pepper to taste
Serve

Notes:

This is not a thick soup, if you wish your soup thicker, simply add a little cornstarch dissolved in cold water and let the soup boil.

Chicken Soup a la Dave

Let anyone in the family get a sniffle and Dave is in the kitchen cooking a pot of chicken soup. The funny thing is that it does seem to work. The first few years we were married I was always surprised and touched to come home from work and find one of his grown kids laying on the couch, waiting for their Dad to make them feel better. That doesn't happen much anymore but the soup is still super.

What you need:

3 cans chicken broth
1 whole chicken, cleaned and rinsed
1 teaspoon salt (only use if chicken broth is low sodium)
Fresh ground pepper to taste

How to assemble:

In a large soup pot simmer chicken in broth for approximately 1 hour

Remove chicken to platter to cool saving all the broth

Place the broth in the refrigerator to cool so fat will congeal on top (Hint: if you're in a hurry you can use a de-fatter)

When chicken is cool enough to handle remove and save all the meat, discarding the skin and bones

Cut chicken in bite size pieces

Remove chilled broth from the refrigerator and remove solid coating of fat on top (discard fat)

Add chicken to broth and simmer another ½ hour before serving.

Variations in serving:

For the sick, serve the broth with or without the chicken accompanied by dry toast or saltine crackers.

Serve for a meal with one of the following:

1. Chicken and Dumplings—use the recipe on the Bisquick box but remember they double in size. Add the dumplings to boiling soup, cook uncovered for 10 minutes then turn the heat down to simmer, cover the pot and continue cooking for 20 minutes. The soup will thicken to a gravy-like consistency and the dumplings will float on top.
2. With vegetables and pasta. Add diced carrots, celery, onions and any other vegetable when you simmer the last ½ hour. 20 minutes before serving add your choice of pasta.
3. Same as above but also add 1 can of stewed tomatoes (including the tomato broth) with the pasta
4. Same as #2 but add diced potatoes with vegetables and eliminate the pasta

Notes:

Curried Corn Soup

I think I mentioned that both of my girls got married recently and as neither are as great at cooking as they are at eating its fortunate that both husbands cook. Danielle's Dave is especially handy in the kitchen and loves to turn out exceptional dishes while Danielle acts as his assistant. This soup came from one of his best friends who first served it to him at a night of bridge and now Dave makes it whenever he can. A bowl makes a meal. Let the soup sit over night in the fridge if you like a stronger curry flavor.

What you need:

4 tablespoons olive oil
1 cup onions, diced
2 tablespoons garlic, minced
1/3 cup carrots, peeled and grated
2 tablespoons fresh ginger, peeled and grated
1/3 cup celery, diced
4 cups potatoes, peeled and cubed
5 cups chicken stock (3 cans)
6 cups corn (4 cans)
2 tablespoons curry powder
1/4 teaspoon turmeric powder
1/4 teaspoon chili powder
1/4 teaspoon cumin, ground
1/8 teaspoon cardamon, ground
1/8 teaspoon fennel seeds, ground
1 cup heavy whipping cream
1 ½ teaspoon salt
pepper to taste

How to assemble:

Heat oil in large soup pot.

Sauté onions, garlic, carrots, ginger and celery over medium heat for 10 minutes.

Add potatoes, stock, 3 cups of corn, curry. turmeric. chili powder, cumin, cardamom and fennel.

Cook 20 minutes over medium heat until the potatoes are tender.

Remove soup from heat and cool.

Blend in food processor, blender or immersion blender until smooth.

Return mixture to soup pot and add remaining corn and whipping cream

Cook over medium flame until heated through

Add salt and pepper to taste.

Serve with croutons and corn sprinkled on top for garnish

Notes:

Dave Limp, Danielle's husband, at work in his kitchen.

Dave's Hot and Sour Turkey Soup

Dave doesn't always make this the day after Thanksgiving the way he did before we were married because, frankly, after that huge meal we just want to get rid of the carcass. But since this is Janet's favorite soup, and he hates to throw away good food, he now boils down the carcass, freezes the broth and makes this soup on another day.

What you need:

Turkey carcass, bones, skin and everything
water
2-3 cans of chicken broth
2 stalks of celery, including leaves if any
1 large onion, quarted
1 large can stewed tomatoes
1 large jar of dill pickles
½ pound of pasta
1/4 teaspoon of garlic granules
Salt and pepper to taste

How to assemble:

In a heavy soup pot put turkey carcass, include all the bones and skin
Add chicken broth and then enough water to just cover the carcass
Add a peeled, quartered onion and the celery
Simmer for 3-4 hours
Remove from fire and pour soup through a strainer into another pan
Put broth in refrigerator to chill

Keep the strainer of vegetables, skin, bones and meat until the
   contents cool
Pick through the strainer and remove all pieces of meat, discard
   the rest
When broth has chilled and the fat has congealed on top, remove
   and discard the fat.
Add the turkey meat salvaged from the strainer to the broth
**Note: This is the point where you can freeze the broth for another
   day or proceed with the soup**

In a large soup pot heat the broth and meat
Add the canned tomatoes
Add approximately 1 cup of dill pickle juice
Add the garlic granules and salt and pepper to taste
Simmer about 1 hour.
Taste soup and adjust seasoning if needed
Add pasta and continue simmering for 20 minutes
Serve

Notes:

A variety of other things can be added to this soup such as
mushrooms, a variety of vegetables, and you could use rice or
potatoes instead of pasta.

French Onion Soup

Winter calls for soup and this is one of my favorites. I don't know why I never made it earlier in my cooking career but I think I assumed it was too difficult. But one day I was watching Martha Stewart and she made it. I realized how easy it was. I didn't bother to write down her recipe because as everyone who knows me knows, I always think I can do anything as well, if not better, than anyone else. And maybe this soup proves it.

Don't be afraid of making the whole recipe because you can freeze the excess in Baggies and get it out of the freezer whenever you have a yen.

What you need:

3 lbs of brown onions and at least one sweet onion, i.e. Walla
    Walla or Maui onion
8 cups of rich beef broth (made from scratch, canned, from Au Jus
    powder or a combination of all of them)
½ lb bacon
½ cup of dry vermouth
1 teaspoon salt
Fresh ground pepper to taste
1/4 teaspoon of dried thyme or 1 teaspoon of fresh thyme
½ baguette of french or sour dough bread
1 lb Gruyere cheese
Dry Sherry (optional)

How to assemble:

Peel the onions and slice thinly

In a large soup pot cook the bacon until crisp

Remove the bacon to drain on paper towels and add the onions to the bacon fat

Stir occasionally until the onions caramelized to a rich brown and are cooked down to about 1/4 their original size (about 30 to 45 minutes)

Add the vermouth to the pan to deglaze it, this is important to capture all the rich flavor for the soup

Let the vermouth and onions come to a boil to release all the alcohol and then add the beef broth

Add the salt and pepper to taste

Cover and cook for about 30 minutes. Don't overcook as the onions may disintegrate.

Slice bread into ½ inch thick slices and make into croutons by toasting dry under the broiler or in a toaster.

Slice the cheese very thin with a vegetable peeler or grate it coarsely

Crumble the bacon into bits

How to serve:

Turn on broiler

Arrange soup bowls on a baking sheet (make sure you're using bowls that are oven proof)

Add 1 tablespoon of Dry Sherry to the bottom of each bowl (optional)

Place one or two croutons in the bottom of the bowl

Sprinkle bacon bits on top of crouton

Ladle hot soup on the crouton until bowl is reasonably full

Lay sliced or grated cheese over the top

Put baking sheet of bowls under the broiler until the cheese bubbles and browns

Serve immediately

Notes:

Use a variety of onions for best results but include one or two sweet onions such as Maui or Walla Walla to ensure the best carmelization. If no sweet onions are available add a teaspoon or two of granulated sugar in the pot when carmelizing the onions.

Gazpacho

This cold, refreshing soup is wonderful on a hot summer day. I had tried it at various restaurants and then one hot summer day I turned an abundance of produce from my garden into this winner. I've made it since but now I just buy the ingredients at the local Farmers' Market.

What you need:

6 ripe, large tomatoes
1 large bell pepper
1 large cucumber
4-6 green onions
2 stalks of celery and/or 1 small zucchini (zucchini is optional)
3 cups V-8 juice
1/4 cup Wishbone Italian Dressing (or similar)
½ teaspoon salt
pinch of cayenne pepper (or to taste but be careful, it should only have a slight bite)
2 tablespoon fresh lemon juice
handful of fresh cilantro sour cream for garnish

How to assemble:

Clean and finely chop all the vegetables (I use my Cusinart for this)
Assemble the vegetables and the V-8 juice in a large bowl
Add Italian dressing, lemon juice, salt, pepper and 1 tablespoon of finely chopped cilantro

Mix contents and taste, adjust seasonings to taste

Chill at least three hours before serving

Pour in bowls and garnish with a dollop of sour cream and a few
cilantro leaves

Serve with tortilla chips

This dish will keep for several days in the refrigerator, it is low in
calories and fat, refreshing and nutritious

Notes:

Poblamo Pepper Soup

Dave and I have gone to San Miguel de Allende, Mexico a couple of times. It's a lovely place in the mountains about 100 miles north of Mexico City. One day we took a drive up in the mountains and had lunch at a very nice restaurant with a wonderful view. Dave had this soup. When we got back he couldn't rest until he duplicated it. This is the result of his efforts and one which we all enjoy.

What you need:

4-5 Poblamo peppers (if you don't know what they look like ask your produce supplier)
2 quarts chicken broth
1 medium size brown onion
1 tablespoon butter or olive oil
½-1 pint sour cream

How to assemble:

Turn your oven on to broil
Peel and dice onion and saute in a frying pan until tender, then set aside
Put the chicken broth in large soup pot and begin to heat
Wash and split the peppers, removing **all seeds** and stems
Lay the peppers on a baking sheet cut side down, skin side up
Place the baking sheet under the broiler and cook until the skins are blackened and blistered
Remove peppers and cool to point they can be handled
Remove all skin

Dice pepper into small pieces

Using a blender, add some peppers, some onions and a small amount of hot broth and process to puree stage

Pour puree in another pan and repeat until all peppers and onions have been processed

Add the remaining chicken broth to the pepper puree and mix well

Simmer about 45 minutes

Before serving, remove from fire

When soup has stopped bubbling stir in the sour cream

Serve immediately

Notes:

Pumpkin-Leek Bisque

The Nut Tree was a famous landmark on the highway between San Francisco and Sacramento until only a few years ago. Anytime I went that way I stopped there for a break, to browse through their shops and sometimes to eat. It was a pretty pricy dining room but that only served to make those occasions I ate there more special. They served a wonderful pumpkin soup at dinner that I'm always trying to match. This recipe is very close.

What you need:

3 large leeks, rinsed well and sliced thin
1 tablespoon butter
2 cups chicken broth
2 cups water
2 cups canned pumpkin
½ cup half and half
½ teaspoon nutmeg
1/8 teaspoon cayenne pepper

How to assemble:

In a heavy soup pot saute the leeks in butter until the leeks are
    tender
Add broth, water and pumpkin and simmer 10 minutes
Add the half and half, nutmeg and cayenne pepper and simmer
    another 10 minutes
Serve

Notes:

Spicy Pumpkin Bisque

As long as we're talking Pumpkin Bisque, here's another with a totally different taste. Pumpkin can be used for other purposes than pie or bread and this soup is unusual and tasty.

What you need:

1/4 cup olive oil
1 medium onion, chopped
2 large carrots, coarsely chopped
1 ½ teaspoon dried mustard
1 teaspoon cumin
½ teaspoon turmeric
½ teaspoon ginger
½ teaspoon cinnamon
1/8 teaspoon cayenne
3 cups chicken broth
1 1/3 cups cooked and mashed pumpkin (you can use canned)
1 1/4 cans half and half
1 cup dry white wine

How to assemble:

In a heavy soup pot saute onions in the oil until onions are soft (about 7 minutes)
Add carrots and spices, continuing to saute until carrots are tender (about 10 minutes more)
Add stock and pumpkin, cover and simmer about 15 minutes
Remove from heat and cool slightly
Using a blender, puree small about of broth and vegetables at a

time
Return puree to a pot and heat over moderate heat
Pour in cream
When soup is hot but not boiling add wine
Cook for 5 minutes more without boiling
Serve immediately

Notes:

Teresa's Tortilla Soup

Dave and I drove across country from Houston to the West Coast stopping to visit family and friends and when we arrived in Temecula to stay with Teresa and her family this soup was already in the making. We love tortilla soup and this was so exceptional we ate it for lunch the next day but alas, then it was gone. Make it for yourself and enjoy.

What you need:

4 chopped, cooked chicken breasts
2 cans Diced Tomatoes & Green Chilies (10 OZ, Ro-Tel, mild)
2 small cans Ortega chopped green chilies mild
2 cans tomato soup
2 cans water
1 onion chopped
1 clove garlic chopped
4 cans of chicken broth
1 large can pinto beans, drained salt and pepper to taste
1 tablespoon chili powder (or to taste)
1 bag tortilla strips
½ pint sour cream
1 cup shredded cheese

How to assemble:

Poach skinless, boneless chicken breasts in 1 can of chicken broth
Remove chicken and cool, chop or shred to be added later to soup
Set aside chicken broth
Saute onions and garlic

Add to pan of chicken broth
Add all other ingredients except for the chicken and beans
Simmer for 1 hour
Add chicken and beans and simmer 15 minutes

Serve with shredded cheese, sour cream and tortilla chips to sprinkle
on top of soup.

Notes:

You could use a whole chicken, cool and throw away skin and bones, using meat and broth for soup.

If you like your soup a little thicker substitute a can of refried beans for the pinto beans.

Zucchini Soup

Ahh, the dreaded zucchini. If I was going to cook zucchini this is one of the ways I would consider serving it. I found this recipe in my last days of dealing with my zucchini crop and we actually liked it. Unfortunately, while our zucchini overload is more mental than it is physical, it will still be a while before you'll be served this soup at our house. But you might like to try it at yours.

What you need:

2 tablespoons butter or margarine
2 medium onions chopped
4 cups chicken stock
2 cups fresh zucchini cubed
½ teaspoon salt pepper to taste

How to assemble:

In a heavy soup pan saute the onion in the butter until they start
    to brown
Pour in the chicken stock, the zucchini, the salt and pepper
Bring to a boil
Lower the fire so soup will simmer
When zucchini is tender remove the pot from the fire and cool
When soup is cool, puree a couple of cups at a time in the blender
When all the soup is pureed, return it to the soup pot
Heat to almost boiling and serve

Notes:

Broccoli Salad

Have trouble getting your family to eat broccoli? Here's a healthy salad that perks up a buffet table.

What you need:

4 cups of broccoli florets
1/4 cup raisins
1/4 cup of chopped white onion
8 strips of bacon, cooked crisp and crumbled
3/4 cup mayonnaise
1/4 cup sugar
2 tablespoons of white or cider vinegar

How to assemble:

Dressing:
Mix sugar, vinegar and mayonnaise and stir well

Salad:
Zap the broccoli in the microwave for about a minute until its still
    a vivid green and crunchy
Place the broccoli in a good sized bowl
Add the chopped onions, raisins and crumbled bacon
Toss in the dressing
Serve

If you have leftovers, relax as this salad keeps well in the refrigerator
for 2 or 3 days

Notes:

Caesar Salad

I moved to San Francisco in 1964. It was my big adventure. Of course I didn't know anyone and I was very poor for a long time but I still loved it. None of the people I met could really afford to go out to dinner so we took turns playing host. I liked to cook and I tried all kinds of recipes. One of my friends from Nevada gave me this recipe and I thought I was hot stuff. Gourmet at least. Anyway, it is good and it was very popular. I would make it more often but it wastes the leftover anchovies. I can't bear to throw them away so they sit in the refrigerator until they get really gross. On reflection I think I should make more of the lemon juice with anchovies and then freeze it in little Baggies, then I would only have to defrost and add the green onions.

What you need:

1 lemon
3 green onions
2 anchovies
1 head of Romaine lettuce
2-3 tablespoons of olive oil
2 teaspoons wine vinegar
1 egg
½ cup of croutons
1/4 cup Parmesan cheese, grated

How to assemble:

Squeeze lemon juice into a small bowl removing any seeds
Finely chop the green onions and add to juice
Chop the anchovy fillets and add to lemon and green onions
Let set for 1 or more hours to neutralize and blend the flavors
Wash and dry the lettuce discarding any tougher outside leaves
Break the remaining leaves into small pieces and put in a large salad bowl. (Never cut the leaves always break them apart with your hands)
Toss the leaves with a small amount of olive oil until they are coated but not drowned
Add the vinegar and continue tossing
Add the lemon juice and toss—beware, if you taste it now you'll find it very sour
Beat the egg with a little salt and pepper until frothy
Pour the egg, croutons and cheese on the salad
Toss and serve immediately

Notes:

Chinese Chicken Salad

This a great addition to a pot luck, a special buffet or it can even be a light summer meal. It can be made with either iceberg lettuce or cabbage and is good either way. Anytime you have leftover chicken, fried, teriyaki or even baked you have the main ingredient for this salad.

What you need:

Dressing:
2 tablespoons of sugar
3 tablespoons of white or cider vinegar
1/3 cup minus 1 tablespoon of light oil
1 tablespoon sesame oil
1 seasoning packet from Top Ramen noodles

Salad:
1 medium head of iceberg lettuce or cabbage, shredded finely
2 or 3 green onions
4 oz of slivered, blanched almonds
2 tablespoons sesame seeds
1 cup of diced cooked chicken (more if you want) fresh cilantro
    (optional)
1 package Top Ramen, Chicken Flavored Noodles

How to assemble:

Dressing:
Mix in a jar the sugar, vinegar, oils and the contents of the Seasoning
    Package from the Top Ramen

Shake well and set aside

Salad:
In a large salad bowl place the shredded lettuce or cabbage
Add the chopped green onions, diced chicken and the fresh cilantro
leaves (optional)
Crumble the dried noodles from the Top Ramen package and add
to salad
Sprinkle in the sesame seed
Shake the dressing one more time and pour over the salad
Toss well so all salad is coated
Sprinkle almonds on top with a few more cilantro leaves for garnish
Serve

Notes:

This salad made with cabbage can be refrigerated for two or
three days if you have leftovers. While the noodles will lose their
crispiness the cabbage still gives it a pleasing crunch.

This salad made with lettuce needs to be served and eaten
within hours of making it.

Connie's Strawberry Jello Mold

I thought I made this up years ago but stopped serving it when the grandkids didn't eat it. Their mothers' said it had too many things in it, so I switched to plain Jello. A couple of years ago my little sister, Teresa, and her family came to Thanksgiving at our house and she brought this dish. Everyone raved about it and wanted the recipe. She said she got it from Connie and so now I serve it again but it's Connie's Strawberry Jello Mold.

What you need:

1 large package of Strawberry Jello
2 cups boiling water
2 8oz containers of strawberry yogurt
1 small box of frozen strawberries, thawed
2 cups of Cool Whip or equivalent

How to assemble:

Mix Jello in boiling water until completely dissolved
Add the strawberries, mixing well
Carefully stir in the yogurt until it is blended into the Jello and strawberry mixture
Let set until slightly thick and then fold in the Cool Whip
Pour into Jello mold or pretty serving bowl and chill until set

Notes:

Try different flavors:
Cherry Jello with frozen cherries and cherry yogurt
Orange Jello with mandarin oranges and orange yogurt
You get the picture.

Five Cup Salad (Ambrosia)

I have a hard time calling this a salad because it really is more of a desert. But you find this at the best pot lucks and picnics. The kids gleefully help themselves while the parents look the other way pretending its only salad.

What you need:

1 cup mandarin oranges, drained
1 cup crushed pineapple, drained
1 cup miniature marshmallows
1 cup flaked coconut
1 cup sour cream

How to assemble:

Mix together and chill overnight or at least 3 hours before serving

Notes:

Feel free to add other fresh or canned fruits to this dish, such as sweet cherries, apricots or even fresh banana or kiwi would go well.

Four Bean Salad

Here's another of those favorites you find at most picnics or pot lucks. If you're the one who is bringing it, use this recipe and you won't disappoint anyone.

What you need:

1 can green beans
1 can golden wax beans
1 can garbanzo beans
1 can kidney beans
1 red or brown onion
1 green pepper
½ cup white or cider vinegar
½ cup sugar
½ cup oil
salt and pepper to taste

How to assemble:

Drain all the liquid from the cans of beans and combine in a large
    bowl
Peel and thinly slice the onion and add to beans
Core and de-seed the pepper, slicing it into pieces the approximate
    size of the beans and add to bowl
In a separate bowl add the vinegar, sugar and oil and beat thoroughly
Pour over the bean mixture and toss until everything is coated
Add salt and pepper to taste

Refrigerate overnight to allow the flavors to blend
Toss once more before serving

Notes:

Fresh Fruit Salad

It seems silly to include this because there is no set recipe but I may as well explain it for those of you who have committed to bring this dish but have no clue as to how to do it. First of all the fruit needs to be ripe and tasty. Secondly, the types of fruit need to look attractive together and the flavors need to be compatible. For instance, if cherries are in season use a couple of different kinds with a couple kinds of melon, pineapple, kiwi and banana. Strawberries can easily replace the cherries or in the winter you can use apples, oranges, pineapples, grapes and etc. Do not use sour or hard fruit, it tempts no one.

What you need:

5 to 7 kinds of fresh fruit
½ cup fresh orange juice (an alternate can be fresh lemon juice with 1/4 cup of sugar added)

How to assemble:

Peel fruit and cut in similar size pieces
Toss together in a bowl with orange juice
Chill for a couple hours
Toss again just before serving

Notes:

Fruit flavored yogurt or sour cream mixed with orange juice makes a good topping for this salad

My sister, Connie, mixes in a large can of Cherry Pie filling then serves it in a hollowed out pineapple or watermelon. It's attractive and tasty.

Gayle's Signature Green Salad

For years this was the salad I made. Understand, I didn't make it every night, only when I was cooking for company or after I married Dave, I made it frequently for Sunday dinner.

What you need:

2 heads of lettuce (usually one red leaf lettuce and one butter lettuce)
1 ripe avocado
3 green onions
1 medium size tomato
1 cucumber (optional)
6 oz of bay shrimp (sometimes called salad shrimp)
1/4 cup grated Parmesan cheese
Wishbone Italian Dressing (or any good Italian dressing will do)

How to assemble:

Rinse and dry lettuce
In a large salad bowl add the lettuce broken into bite size pieces
Peel and dice the avocado, tomato and cucumber
Chop and add the green onions
Add shrimp
Sprinkle cheese over the top
Put bowl uncovered in the refrigerator for ½ hour before serving to crisp up the lettuce (The cheese will prevent the avocado from turning black)
Just before serving shake the dressing bottle and pour over the salad a little at a time and toss

You want the salad to be covered by the dressing but not drowned in it
Serve

Variations:

Use a variety of lettuces but always at least two
Use crab instead of shrimp
Add croutons
Change dressings
Use a package of Good Seasonings Italian Mix and use lemon juice
    instead of vinegar

Notes:

Leslie's Spinach Salad

Isn't it great when you start getting recipes from the next generation? Leslie is Connie's youngest and she's had years of experience in participating in family events. She started cooking at an early age because she loves to try new things. On her last visit with us she pulled this recipe out of her head and I think, judging by our enthusiastic consumption, it's a winner.

What you need:

12 oz baby spinach leaves washed and dried
4 oz blue cheese, crumbled
2/3 cup dried cranberries (try Ocean Spray Cranraisins)
½ cup sliced, candied Almonds
1 tablespoon butter
1/4 cup brown sugar, packed
½ cup olive oil
2 tablespoons sesame oil
3 tablespoons balsamic vinegar
1 tablespoon Soy Sauce
3 tablespoons white sugar
1 flavor package for Top Ramen Noodles, Chicken Flavored

How to assemble:

Candied Almonds:
In a heavy skillet melt the butter and add the brown sugar
Stirring frequently, when the mixture is thoroughly melted and
    bubbly add the Almonds.

Stir well until the sugar mixture adheres to the nuts then remove from the fire and spread the nuts on an oiled cooking sheet to cool

Salad:

Assemble the spinach, blue cheese, cranberries and Almonds in a salad bowl

In a separate covered container mix the olive oil, sesame oil, vinegar, soy sauce, sugar and flavor package

Shake well

Pour over salad and toss

Serve

Notes:

If you want to use this salad for a whole meal add the crushed Top Ramen Noodles and some chicken to make a different Chicken Salad

Norwegian Spaghetti Salad

This makes a good meal on a hot day or an addition to a buffet. It's simple, nutritious and tasty but I doubt it's really Norwegian. I got it from a Swedish lady.

What you need:

½ lb of uncooked spaghetti
½ cooked shrimp (Bay or Salad shrimp)
1 small package of frozen peas and carrots
1/4 cup of fresh parsley
Salt and Pepper to taste
Dill-Caper Dressing from this book

How to assemble:

Break spaghetti into 3 or 4 pieces and add to salted boiling water
Cook to al dente and then rinse in cold water until cool
Drain and put in large bowl
Rinse peas and carrots under hot water until defrosted, drain and
    add to pasta
Chop parsley and add
Add shrimp
Toss with Dill-Caper Dressing (see recipe in this book)
Salt and pepper to taste
Garnish with Shrimp and parsley
Chill over night

Notes:

Pear and Blue Cheese Salad

I love a good green salad and there are endless variations. This was a salad I had first in the Loire Valley. We had driven out of Paris and our first stop was Amboise. We sat outside in the October sun, in the shade of the castle wall, lunching on omelettes and sharing this salad. No wonder we love it. I have served it many times and I add things and change the ingredients but I still get rave reviews anytime I serve it.

What you need:

1 large or 2 small heads of butter lettuce
1 large ripe pear
1/4 lb blue cheese (Blue Castillo is our favorite)
½ cup walnut or pecan pieces
3 green onions
1 avocado (optional)
olive oil
wine vinegar

How to assemble:

Rinse and drain the lettuce, discarding any tough outer leaves
Break lettuce into bit size pieces into salad bowl
Peel and core pear, cutting it into bite size pieces
Crumble cheese into the bowl
Peel and slice the avocado
Add 1-2 tablespoons of good olive oil, tossing the salad well while
    the oil lightly coats the lettuce

Add 3-4 dashes of wine vinegar and toss again, adding salt and
    pepper to taste

Variations:

Use pre-packaged lettuce mix instead of all butter lettuce
Use apple or orange instead of pear
Saute walnuts or pecans in equal portions of butter and brown
    sugar and allow to crystalize before adding to the salad
If you add orange, omit the avocado and add boiled shrimp
Use a lemon or pear based commercial salad dressing

Notes:

Gayle, Rick and Joni Wall resting at a Paris Café on the
trip to France where we discovered the Pear and Blue
Cheese Salad. We owe Rick and Joni for introducing us,
it was the beginning of a beautiful relationship.

Spinach Salad

When I was a child there was fresh spinach, which my mother never served, and there was canned spinach, which needed all the persuasion Popeye could muster to promote it because even served with lemon juice it was vile. Now, when you can't get fresh, which is hardly ever, you can get frozen, which is good in cooking but hardly appropriate for salads. This is my favorite way to serve spinach but as you'll notice from the recipes in this book there are endless ways to serve it and not one of these recipes calls for canned spinach. The spinach canners have probably gone out of business. Thank god!

What you need:

1 package of prepared fresh spinach or 2 bunches of fresh spinach
2 peeled hard boiled eggs, grated or chopped
½ lb bacon, cooked crisp and crumbled
3 or 4 green onions
Poppy Seed Dressing (see recipe in this section)

How to assemble:

Rinse and dry the spinach leaves then break into bite size pieces
Chop the green onions and add to spinach
Sprinkle egg and bacon on top and place in refrigerator to chill for
    about 15 minutes before serving
Just before serving add enough dressing to lightly coat the leaves

Variations:

Add any combination or all of the following

Avocado, Shrimp, Cubed Chicken, Black Olives, Grated Cheese, Roasted Garlic, Tomatoes and/or Croutons

Notes:

Tomato Aspic Salad

This is a very fancy version of Gazpacho and is wonderful for a nice lunch or a fancy buffet. One of the ladies I worked with when I first came to San Francisco invited a few of us to her house and she served this for lunch. We were so impressed. So much so that I make it myself from time to time.

What you need:

6 ripe, large tomatoes
1 large bell pepper
1 large cucumber
4-6 green onions
2 stalks of celery and/or 1 small zucchini (zucchini is optional)
3 cups V-8 juice
1/4 cup Wishbone Italian Dressing (or similar)
½ teaspoon salt
pinch of cayenne pepper (or to taste but be careful, it should only have a slight bite)
2 tablespoon fresh lemon juice
4 envelopes of Knox Unflavored Gelatine
1 cup of cooked and cleaned shrimp (or salmon, crab or chicken)
handful of fresh cilantro
sour cream for garnish

How to assemble:

Clean and chop all the vegetables and place in a large bowl (I use my Cuisinart for this)
Heat two cups of V-8 juice to boil

Meanwhile place 1 cup of V-8 in a medium size bowl and sprinkle the Gelatine over the juice

When the Gelatine has set approximately 1 minute pour the boiling juice over it and stir until the two are mixed and the Gelatine is dissolved

Pour the juice and Gelatine over the vegetables

Add the Italian Dressing, lemon juice, salt, pepper and 1 tablespoon of chopped fresh cilantro

Fold in Shrimp

Taste the aspic, adjust seasonings if needed

Pour into a ring Jello mold or other decorative mold

Chill until set (usually 3-4 hours)

Just before serving immerse mold quickly in bath of hot water, caution don't get it in the mold, set serving plate on top and then invert the mold on to the serving plate

Garnish with greens and serve with sour cream

Notes:

Vegetable Salad Mold

This was another of Aunt Kate's recipes. She served it to us on one of our visits to her and Phil in Oregon. It goes very well in the summer on a buffet table or with a barbeque. Or use it instead of the traditional cole slaw and watch the reaction.

What you need:

1 small box of Lemon Jello
1 ½ cups water
2 tablespoons minced onion
1 green pepper, seeded and chopped fine
2 cups of finely shredded cabbage
½ cup celery, chopped
½ teaspoon salt
2-3 dashes of cayenne pepper (watch out, too much is too much)
6 oz cream cheese, room temperature
1/4 cup cream (half & half)
1/3 cup mayonnaise

How to assemble:

Make Jello by dissolving it in 3/4 cup boiling water, then adding
    3/4 cup cold water and set aside
Cream together the cream cheese, cream and mayonnaise
In a separate bowl assemble all other ingredients
When Jello has set to a thick syrupy stage stir in the cheese mixture
Stir gently until mixed well
Add all the other ingredients
Pour mixture into a Jello mold or another decorative mold

Chill until set (usually 3-4 hours in the refrigerator)

Just before serving immerse mold quickly in bath of hot water, caution don't get it in the mold, set serving plate on top and then invert the mold on to the serving plate

Garnish with greens and serve

Notes:

Dill-Caper Dressing

This is a great dressing for pasta salads and you can use it as a sauce for crab cakes or salmon, or any fish.

What you need:

3/4 cup mayonnaise
3/4 cup sour cream
2 medium dill pickles, chopped fine
2 tablespoons capers, rinse and drain
4 green onions, chopped fine
1 teaspoon dill
salt and pepper to taste

How to assemble:

Add ingredients together in order they are listed
Mix thoroughtly
Chill overnight or 3-4 hours before serving so flavors will blend

Notes:

Poppy Seed Salad Dressing

Aunt Helen was one of Dad's older sisters and Barb's mother. When Barb moved to the Gold Country, Aunt Helen and Uncle Herman used to visit her annually and they always visited me in San Francisco, for a couple of days either coming or going. She gave me this recipe and it is wonderful. It is sweet and sour and goes very well on any salad but I especially like it on a spinach salad.

What you need:

½ cup Karo Syrup (red label)
1/4 cup white or cider vinegar
1 cup oil
1 tablespoon freshly grated onion with juice
1 teaspoon salt
1 teaspoon dry mustard
1 teaspoon paprika
1 teaspoon poppy seeds

How to assemble:

Blend the syrup, vinegar, onion and spices in a blender
Slowly add the oil while continuing to blend
Drizzle on salad and toss
Store leftovers in the refrigerator but bring to room temperature
and shake well before using

Notes:

For a different taste use celery seeds instead of poppy seeds.

Salad Stuff

You've seen this before, Salad "Something". You use it to sprinkle on buttered bread before browning it in the oven, you sprinkle it on cottage cheese and on salads. Mix this in sour cream for a lively dip. I use it to season flour for my fried chicken. So instead of paying a lot for a small bottle of it in the market, make your own.

What you need:

1 box sesame seeds
½ box celery seeds
½ box poppy seeds
½ cup + 2 tablespoons Parmesan cheese
3/4 teaspoon garlic powder
3/4 teaspoon Accent
1 tablespoon salt
2 tablespoons paprika
1 tablespoon dried chopped parsley

How to assemble:

Mix all ingredients together
Store in air tight container
Keep refrigerated to prevent the cheese from molding

Notes:

Put in a pretty jar and give it as a gift

A Sunday family dinner with Danielle dishing up the
ice cream for Miles, Diane, Nicole, Amy and Shan,
Marc and Rocelle's oldest son.

Vegetables and
Side Dishes

Thanksgiving at Miles and Diane's with Dave, Danielle,
Dave Limp, Miles and Diane's niece, Elaine

CONTENTS

Asparagus Pockets

I came up with this dish one Sunday out of sheer boredom. Everyone loved it. It was a long time before I was able to serve asparagus plain. It isn't much work and somehow it gives your meal a touch of elegance.

What you need:

large can of Pillsbury Crescent Rolls (find them In the dairy section)
fresh asparagus
1 tablespoon butter

How to assemble:

Open the can of crescent rolls and spread them out
Detach and assemble 8 triangles
Break off the woody stems of the asparagus
Rinse and dry the asparagus spears
Place 4 or 5 spears on a triangle (if large 2 or 3 may do), tops
    arranged on the apex
Put a small dot of butter on the base of the asparagus
Fold the two bottom corners over the base of the asparagus, tucking
    the corner in neatly
Place the pockets on a baking sheet and bake according to the
    directions on the package of Crescent Rolls
(If you prefer your asparagus to be more cooked, you can zap it in
    the microwave for 1 minute prior to assembling the pockets

Notes:

Baked or Roasted Potatoes

After all those years of having potatoes with every meal when I was a kid, I kind of went the other way as an adult. I concentrated on meats and salads and usually ignored potatoes, even in restaurants. But I gained a new appreciation of the vegetable after eating Dave's baked potatoes. It's so simple but different and delicious. I included my roasted potatoes for a change but you'll never go wrong with his.

What you need:

2 medium potatoes per person or one large per person

If making roasted potatoes:

butter
salt and pepper

How to assemble:

Peel and rinse the potatoes

Baked Potatoes:
If the potatoes are large cut them in half
Bake in a pre-heated oven to 350° for 1 hour
Using tongs, turn the potatoes over after the first ½ hour
Do not use a fork or puncture the potatoes until they are done
When the potatoes are brown and crisp on the outside use a fork
    to puncture them to release the steam, serve immediately with

your favorite fixings, butter, sour cream, cheese sauce, bacon bits, chopped green onions or etc.

Roasted Potatoes:
Cut medium potatoes into about 4 chunks
Lay the chunks on a baking sheet
Place a dab of butter on each piece
Sprinkle with salt and pepper
Bake in a pre-heated oven to 350° for 1 hour
Turn the potatoes over after the first ½ hour
Remove and serve

Notes:

Basic Marinara

I started making this when my gardening efforts left me with a profusion of tomatoes. After the first year of using my own marinara I couldn't find any commercial sauce to satisfy me so the next year I didn't depend on my gardening skills and the fickle drought pattern I just went to the Farmers' Market and bought the ingredients I needed.

I never know how much I will need in a year so I make lots, freeze it in a variety of container sizes and give it away if I have too much. I use this for the beginning of all kinds of dishes including lasagne, ravioli and spaghetti sauce.

Make this in late August or September, whenever the tomatoes are in profusion. Do not buy your tomatoes from the grocery stores. Those tomatoes are picked green and do not develop the flavor you need for this sauce. Grow your own, strike up a friendship with a neighborhood gardener, go to the Farmers' Market or take a drive to the country to buy at a roadside stand, then you're ready to cook.

What you need:

10 lbs tomatoes
2-3 lbs brown onions
2-3 lbs sweet pepper, any type or color
1 head garlic
½ bottle of Spice Islands Italian Herbs (maybe more)
2 teaspoons salt
1 tablespoon sugar
1 teaspoon cayenne pepper
3 tablespoons olive oil

These measurements are not science, a bit more, a bit less won't make that much difference.

How to assemble:

Use a very large heavy kettle and spray liberally with PAM
Smash the garlic, remove the skin and chop the bulbs
Saute the garlic in olive oil
Meanwhile, peel and coarsely chop the onions, adding them to the kettle
Stir occasionally to prevent the garlic and onions from burning
Rinse, core and chop the sweet peppers
Add the peppers to the browned onions and garlic
Wash and core the tomatoes
Cut each one in two and fill the bowl of your Cuisinart or Blender, chop until no large pieces remain and add to kettle
Continue this process until all tomatoes are now in the kettle
At this point the kettle shouldn't be more than ½ filled, if it is, switch to a larger kettle
Add the sugar, salt, pepper and Italian Herbs
Stir and then let simmer without a lid for 3-4 hours
Check occasionally and stir to prevent sticking to the bottom or scorching
After about 3 hours of cooking, taste to see if you need more spices (I sometimes need to add more salt, garlic granules, Italian Herbs, or etc. at this point)
Continue simmering until sauce is thick and rich
Remove from the heat, cover and refrigerate over night
The next day taste the sauce again, add appropriate spices if needed, then store in freezer containers, marked for future use and store in the freezer.

Notes:

Because you cook this sauce uncovered, if the pot is more that ½ full you're liable to spatter sauce all over you kitchen. Save yourself some grief and use a big enough pot.

Cabbage Strudel

This may not sound as wonderful as it is but I urge you try it. Sometimes you can make an ordinary meal truly special with the addition of just one unusual dish. It takes a little time to prepare and while you can prepare the filling in advance you have to assemble the strudel just before baking so its best to not make it for more than 6-8 people.

What you need:

4 cups of cabbage, finely shredded
2 cups of bok choy greens, finely shredded
1 large onion, peeled and sliced thin
2 green onions, chopped
2 tablespoons fresh dill, chopped, or 1 teaspoon dried dill
2 tablespoons fresh parsley, chopped or 1 teaspoon of dried parsley
   flakes
1 teaspoon salt
½ lb of sliced mushrooms
1 teaspoon fresh lemon juice
1 cube butter or margarine
4 large Phyllo pastry sheets (buy in frozen bread sections of most
   markets)
4 tablespoons bread crumbs

How to assemble:

Preparing Filling:
Melt 1 tablespoon of butter in a heavy pan
Saute cabbage, bok choy and onions until greens begin to wilt

Add dill, parsley and salt

Cook for about 1 minute over high heat, stirring frequently

Remove from heat and set aside

Melt 1 tablespoon of butter in a skillet

Add mushrooms and saute over high heat until mushrooms begin to soften

Remove from heat, sprinkle with lemon juice and add to cabbage mixture stirring well

Strain vegetable, removing all liquid and set aside

Preparing Strudel:

Melt the remaining butter

Lay 2 sheets of defrosted Phyllo dough on top of each other on a flat surface

Spead lightly with melted butter

Sprinkle 2 tablespoons of bread crumbs over the surface

Fold the dough in half forming a rectangle

Brush the top lightly with melted butter

Spread ½ the vegetable filling mixture along the long edge of the rectangle stopping 1" from each end.

Fold in the ends of the short sides, encasing the vegetables

Roll the dough around the vegetables as you would a jelly roll

Place the seam side down on a buttered baking sheet

Repeat this process for the second roll

Use the remaining butter to brush the top of each roll

Bake in a pre-heated oven at 400° for about 30 minutes or until the roll is golden brown

Remove from the oven and cut each roll into 3 or 4 pieces and serve

Notes:

Candied Sweet Potatoes

The first time our new daughter-in-law, Rocelle came for Thanksgiving, she offered to bring the sweet potatoes. Now I never much cared for sweet potatoes so I seldom served them but I didn't want to offend her the first time out. How was I to know I never really knew sweet potatoes, having only experienced the "out of the can, covered with marshmallows" kind. I am now addicted to Rocelle's sweet potatoes and I'm not alone. If you want these potatoes the easiest way to get them is to invite Rocelle to dinner. She is always very generous in contributing to the meal. But if for some reason she's not available and you NEED these potatoes, she has very kindly shared her recipe.

What you need:

4 large sweet potatoes, sliced very thin
3 to 4 pints heavy whipping cream
3/4 lb brown sugar
2 tablespoons cinnamon
1/4 teaspoon salt
1 teaspoon nutmeg
1 tablespoon vanilla

How to assemble:

Peel the potatoes and slice thin
Cover the potatoes with water until ready to use
Stir the rest of ingredients together, taking care not to whip the heavy cream

Drain and blot the water from the sweet potatoes

Layer sweet potatoes and cream mixture in a baking dish sprayed with PAM

Bake in a pre-heated oven at 400° for 3 hours or until the cream has carmelized

Notes:

Put a baking sheet under the pan to catch the drips

Rocelle, Sydney and Taylor, Marc's wife and daughters,
at our Wine and Cheese Party

Chinese Fried Rice

I know you can order this in any Chinese restaurant but it's really a dish made to use up leftovers. In fact, you need to start with leftover rice or make the rice the day ahead. Anyway, whether ordered at a restaurant or made at home this dish has endless varieties and is good for a whole meal or as a side to almost any meal.

What you need:

3 cups of cooked, chilled white rice

2 tablespoons oil

1 cup chopped cooked meat (chicken, pork, beef, shrimp, ham or any combination)

½ cup chopped green onions

½ cup green peas or chopped broccoli or Chinese greens

1 egg, beaten

1 tablespoon soy sauce

How to assemble:

Use a wok or large heavy skillet

Heat oil and add rice

Fry and turn for about 15 minutes until some of the rice starts to brown

Add meat, onions and vegetables and continues stirring

Clear a space in the middle of the pan and pour in the egg

Let the egg cook until set and then mix into the rice, continuing to stir

Add the Soy Sauce and stir once more
Serve

Notes:

Cranberry Cherry Relish

Grandma Janet always contributed the fresh cranberry relish to our Thanksgiving dinner and after she was gone I was back to using canned. I found this recipe in the paper and tried it. It converted Dave. He never ate cranberries and now he loves this sauce. He will even add it to his turkey sandwich on occasion just like us gourmands do.

What you need:

2 bags of fresh cranberries (24 ozs.)
3 cups sugar
3/4 cup fresh orange juice
3/4 cup of cranberry juice
zest of one large orange
1 ½ cup of dried cherries

How to assemble:

Prepare the orange zest by grating the orange skin of the fruit leaving only the white on the orange. Use the fine grating side of the grater.

Wash the cranberries, picking through them and discarding any bad ones

Combine all the above ingredients EXCEPT THE CHERRIES in a large heavy pot

Bring to a boil stirring occasionally

Lower to a simmer and cook about 10 minutes or until the berries start popping open

Remove from the heat

Using a metal spoon, skim off foam and discard
Stir in cherries and let mixture cool
Pour into a serving bowl and refrigerate over night or 3-4 hours
This relish keeps in the refrigerator for a month if it last that long.

Notes:

Cranberry Chutney

One of the ladies I worked with listened to me brag about my Cranberry Cherry Relish and she gave me this recipe. It's a different way to serve your cranberries and it's delicious. You might want to experiment. I promise not to feel hurt if you prefer this one.

What you need:

1 bag fresh cranberries
2 tart apples, Granny Smith or Pippin
1 pear, slightly ripe
½ cup golden raisins
1 cup sugar
½ cup fresh orange juice
1 teaspoon cinnamon
1/4 teaspoon nutmeg
1/4 cup Grand Marnier Liquor

How to assemble:

Peel and dice the apples and pear into cubes a little larger than the cranberries
Wash the cranberries and pick through them discarding any bad ones
Combine all the above ingredients EXCEPT THE GRAND MARNIER in a large heavy pot
Bring to a boil stirring occasionally
Reduce heat and simmer uncovered for 45 minutes. Chutney should be thick
Remove from heat

Let cool to warm and then stir in the Grand Marnier Refrigerate covered, until serving.

Notes:

Cukes and Onions in Sour Cream

My mother loved this dish and she would make it for any occasion, picnics, pot lucks, holidays and even extended family dinners. She felt she needed people to share it because two things my father would never eat were cucumbers and onions. It is a very refreshing dish and goes very well with mashed potatoes or even served with bread and butter. Try putting them on top of your next burger, hmmmm.

What you need:

2 medium to large cucumbers
2 medium to large onions
2 tablespoons white or cider vinegar
1 pint sour cream
4 tablespoons salt
Fresh ground pepper to taste

How to assemble:

Peel and thinly slice both the cucumbers and the onions, keeping them separate

In a medium bowl layer cucumber slices, then onion slices, sprinkling each generously with the salt

Repeat this process until all cucumber and onion slices are used

Cover with plastic wrap and let set at room temperature for 2 hours

Thoroughly rinse the vegetables, removing all salt but leaving the layers intact

Drain off all the water

Mix the vinegar, sour cream and pepper together

Pour over the slices of cucumber and onion, do not mix
Cover and chill in the refrigerator over night or for at least 3 hours
before serving.

Notes:

Dave's Rice Pilaf

Dave is the expert here and we never have enough because everyone wants leftovers to take home. While it is excellent as vegetarian or with beef flavor he usually makes it with chicken broth.

What you need:

1 cup white rice
1 medium brown onion, chopped
4 or 5 green onions, chopped
1/4 lb fresh mushrooms, chopped
2 tablespoon olive oil
1 teaspoon salt
2 cups hot chicken broth

How to assemble:

Heat oil in big skillet
Saute rice, onions and mushrooms until rice becomes transparent
Add the broth and salt
Bring contents to boil
Boil mixture until liquid is at the same level as the rice and craters
    in the rice form
Reduce heat to low, cover pot and cook for 20 minutes
DO NOT REMOVE COVER UNTIL TWENTY MINUTES ARE
    UP

Remove from fire and let set until serving. If the pan lid is still hot its ready to serve.

This recipe serves about five so increase it accordingly.

Notes:

Dirty Rice

Rocelle introduced this to our family and contrary to it's name it is a popular dish. It is a well known Cajun recipe and recently some of the more "in" restaurants have been featuring it on the menu. None of theirs is any better than Rocelle's.

What you need:

2-3 tablespoon of olive oil
1 lb of mushrooms, cleaned and thinly sliced
1 large green pepper (sweet) cored, seeded and chopped
2 large onions, peeled and chopped
4 stalks celery, chopped
3 tablespoon minced garlic
1 lb each of mild and hot pork sausage
½ lb each of chicken livers and gizzards boiled until tender and
    chopped fine
5 cups *cooked* white rice
garlic
salt and pepper to taste
parsley, chopped for garnish

How to assemble:

Heat oil in heavy large skillet
Saute all vegetables together until lightly wilted
Add sausage broken into small chunks and brown
Add gizzards and livers to pan
Season with garlic salt and pepper

Simmer until sausage is cooked through and all liquid had been
  reduced
Add cooked rice and mix well
Cook until the entire dish is heated well and mixed thoroughly
Garnish with parsley before serving

Notes:

Easy Polenta

When I was a child my mother would occasionally cook something we called mush. It took a long time stirring and boiling until finished and we ate it like oatmeal with sugar and milk. We all loved it and had to eat several bowls. If there was any left on the next day my mother would slice the congealed mush thinly and then fry it crisp. This was served with butter and syrup for breakfast. So every time we had it we were torn between having that one more bowl or abstaining to make sure there would be enough for fried mush the next morning.

Why didn't my mother cook it more often if we like it so much? Why didn't she stir up a batch in the afternoon to congeal for the next day's breakfast? It is one of those mysteries based on her rules. She only made it for dinner (maybe for those days when it was impossible to stretch the food budget any further) and only fried the leftovers.

Fortunately now days mush is polenta, very popular in my household for dinner, breakfast and lunch if it makes it that far. I always double what I think I'll need because leftovers disappear easily.

This recipe is so easy that it's a crime not to make it often. I serve it with marinara, meats or fish. Its wonderful with lamb shanks or ossa buco. Or, just eat it with milk and sugar.

I use Italian Polenta which is really just coarsely ground yellow corn meal. Any will do. And I use special baking dishes I made for polenta, about 4 inches high with a flat bottom and looking good to serve it in. Any Pyrex, ceramic or metal baking dish would do as well.

What you need:

(Serves 6 but I make this much for 4 people)
1 cup polenta (corn meal)
3 1/4 cups lukewarm water
1 teaspoon salt
1 tablespoon butter

How to assemble:

Pre-heat oven to 350°
Place all the ingredients except the butter in the baking dish already
    sprayed with PAM
Stir with a fork until blended than bake, uncovered, for 50 minutes
Add lump of butter and stir with fork
Bake ten more minutes
Serve with a lump of butter melting on top

Variations:

When stirring after cooking for 50 minutes add one or more of the
    following:
    ½ cup grated cheese, Asiago, Parmesan or Romano
    chopped green onions
    basil, rosemary, cilantro or other favorite herbs
    sauteed mushrooms
    can of creamed corn
I know people who make this with milk or chicken broth instead
    of the water and swear by the results.

Experiment and find your own perfect recipe.

Notes:

Fresh String Beans

Whether you've grown them or bought them at a Farmer's Market, string beans are delicious. But if you want to try something different to tempt the taste buds try cooking them this way. I hate to admit it but you could use frozen beans in this recipe if you had to.

What you need:

3 cups string bean pieces
½ lb bacon
1 medium onion, chopped
1 tablespoon butter
1 teaspoon salt
½ teaspoon pepper

How to assemble:

Fry bacon crisp and remove to paper towel to drain fat
Pour off grease
While the bacon was cooking you should wash beans removing
    stems and strings
Break the beans into pieces about 1 ½ inches long
Heat butter in the frying pan
Add onion and saute until onion begins to carmelize
Add string beans, salt and pepper and stir so onion and beans are
    mixed
Cover pot and reduce heat
Cook about 15 minutes, beans should be tender but not limp

Transfer to a serving dish
Crumble bacon over top of beans
Serve

Notes:

Green Chili Casserole

This is a great favorite of the Coates' extended family and you'll find it on all holiday buffets, picnics and even family dinners. My mother started making this before I even moved away from home and since then you'll see that someone has made it for every major event.

What you need:

1 lb grated Jack cheese (approximately 3 cups grated)
½ lb grated sharp Cheddar cheese (approximately 1 ½ cups grated)
8 oz of canned whole mild green chiles
1 tablespoon of butter
2 tablespoons of flour
8 eggs, beaten
1 small can of evaporated milk
salt and pepper to taste

How to assemble:

Butter a casserole dish approximately 9 x 13"
Remove chiles from cans, spread open each chili removing most of
     the seeds—the more seeds the hotter (picante) the dish
Layer the bottom of the casserole with ½ the chiles
Spread ½ the cheese over the chiles
Sprinkle the flour over the first layer
Dot with butter
Use the second ½ of the chiles to make another layer
Use the rest of the cheese on top
Beat the eggs until frothy

Add the milk, salt and pepper and stir well

Pour over the casserole

Put the dish on a baking sheet to catch drips and put in a pre-heated oven at 400° for 15 minutes

Turn the oven down to 350° and bake for 30 minutes or until a knife inserted in the middle comes out clean

Remove from oven and cool about 10 minutes before serving

This can be served hot, lukewarm and its even good cold

Notes:

Kate's Potato Pancakes

As I mentioned before Aunt Kate and Uncle Phil used to visit me frequently and after they moved to Oregon I visited them. Aunt Kate was a great cook and loved to share her recipes. I was an eager recipient. I loved potato pancakes but had very little luck making them until this recipe.

Remember that potato pancakes need to be made and eaten at the same time so you can't make them ahead. Also, I find if I grate the potatoes in the Cuisinart and keep the grated potato in cold water until I'm ready to use them they don't turn brown. Of course, you have to drain them and pat them dry before adding them to the batter but its worth it.

I serve these pancakes with soup for a great meal.

What you need:

4 large potatoes, peeled
2 eggs
1 tablespoon of flour
1 small onion
1 teaspoon salt
1 teaspoon pepper
2 tablespoons butter or oil

How to assemble:

Grate the potatoes and keep submerged in cold water
Grate the onion and put it in a mixing bowl
Beat in eggs, flour and salt and pepper

Thoroughly drain the grated potatoes and pat dry with a paper
   towel
Add potato to egg mixture and stir
Drop by spoonfuls into hot oil or butter in the skillet
Fry until brown and crispy on the edges
Turn and fry the other side
Serve immediately with sour cream and apple sauce garnish

Notes:

Make Ahead Mashed Potatoes

One of the problems in putting together a grand meal is getting everything done and on the table on time. This is especially true on Thanksgiving where typically the turkey is being carved, the gravy is being made, the potatoes are being mashed and someone is trying to dish up all the other parts of the meal. My sister usually has about fifty people for dinner that day and she needs all the help she can get to simplify the process of putting the meal on the table. This recipe was a godsend for her. Not only can you make it up to a week ahead of the meal but it can be cooked in a crock pot so it doesn't even have to use space in the oven. These potatoes are good enough to have any time, not just when you need to save time.

What you need:

This is not enough for fifty, but probably enough for 10

5 lbs potatoes peeled and quartered
2 egg whites, slightly beaten
8 oz cream cheese, room temperature, cut into chunks
½ cup heavy whipping cream
½ cup sour cream
½ cup butter, cut into chunks (1 cube)
1 teaspoon salt
1 teaspoon pepper
1 teaspoon garlic granules

How to assemble:

Boil potatoes in salted water for 40 minutes or until a fork inserted finds them tender

Drain the water off the potatoes

Use a heavy mixer to fluff potatoes

Add butter, cream cheese, salt, pepper and garlic and continue
mixing

Add cream and sour cream and continue whipping

Add beaten egg whites and mix until potatoes are smooth and
creamy

Spoon potatoes into a baking dish or a crock pot liner that has
been sprayed with PAM

Cover and refrigerate until time to cook for meal

Serving Instructions:

3 ½ hours prior to serving insert liner of crock pot in pot and turn
dial to low

Or

45 minutes to serving bake covered dish in pre-heated oven at
350°

In either case, uncover, place on the table with a dab of butter
melting in the center of the potatoes

Notes:

For variety you can add cheese, chives, roasted garlic or anything
that sounds good to you to these potatoes.

*My sister, Connie and her husband, Bob. Their 25
grandchildren make their family gatherings incredible*

Mashed Potatoes

Our family is crazy about mashed potatoes and Janet most of all. Therefore, she has become the master of the mashed potatoes at our house. On Thanksgiving she recruits the little kids to peel the 10 pounds or so of potatoes we cook and then she cooks and mashes them to perfection. I wasn't going to include this recipe because it is so basic I thought everyone already knows how to do this. But then I remembered that even Janet spent a couple of years under Dave's careful tutelage and if you've never cooked something it's neither basic nor easy. So follow this recipe and relax, your potatoes will be wonderful.

What you need:

10 lbs of potatoes, peeled and cut in quarters
½ lb butter (maybe more)
2 cups milk (approximate)
1 teaspoon salt
1 teaspoon pepper

How to assemble:

Boil the potatoes in salted water for about 40 minutes or until a fork inserted in a potato finds it tender
Drain the potatoes completely
Using a heavy duty mixer fluff the potatoes, this means you beat them dry so they are in fluffy little pieces (You may want to do this in two batches of about 5 lbs each)
Cut the butter in chunks and add with salt and pepper to the potatoes, continue beating

Slowly add the milk as you continue beating until the potatoes are smooth and creamy. Be careful not to add too much milk. You want the potatoes to be able to mound and too much milk will make them soupy.

Taste and add more salt and pepper if necessary

Spoon into serving bowl(s) and put a glob of butter on top to melt

Serve

Variations:

If you like flavored potatoes add roasted garlic, chives or grated cheese at the end and stir well.

Notes:

Don't get paranoid about lumps, judging by the mashed potatoes so popular in all the better restaurants, lumps are in.

Mom's Baked Beans

My sister, Connie, told me I couldn't leave this one out. What's a picnic without a dish of baked beans? And this is the recipe my Mom used as she was the one who always brought the baked beans. Mom and Dad engineered many picnics, especially in those early years in California, for two reasons. The first reason is they never got over their awe of the balmy weather and what better way to show it off than to have a feast in one of the beautiful parks. The second reason was space. They were the first ones of a huge family to move to California and over the years all the friends and relatives and their kids came to visit. There were lots of them and there was lots of us. We didn't have enough table space, chairs, utensils and etc. to accommodate all those people so the park was the answer.

It seemed like in those days we could put together a delightful picnic in a very short time. A call to all the relatives that had moved to California, an agreement of where and when to meet and everyone just seemed to be able to throw together the menu. For us kids it was wonderful, it didn't have to be in summer, it might even be on a school night, but that evening we'd be in a park, playing with our cousins and friends, eating great food and enjoying the grown up talk going on around the picnic benches. Life seemed simple and good. And I hope our grandkids feel the same way about our family get-togethers.

What you need:

3 large cans pork and beans (16oz cans, Mom used Hunts because
    they had more beans and less juice, she said)
½ cup brown sugar, packed
1/4 cup spiced, prepared mustard

3/4 cup catsup
1/4 cup molasses
1/4 cup chopped onions
1/8 cup white or cider vinegar
1 teaspoon garlic granules
4 slices of raw bacon

How to assemble:

Drain at least half of the juice from each can of beans
In a large mixing bowl mix all the ingredients but the bacon
Spray a large baking dish with PAM and then add beans
Lay raw bacon over the top
Bake in a pre-heated oven at 350° for 1 hour
Reduce the heat to 250° and bake one additional hour
Remove from oven and serve

Notes:

One of our famous picnics on Easter, probably in 1953.
Standing is Pete, Lee's brother, Uncle Lee holding Nicky,
Dad with Cliff in front of him, Aunt Nell, Aunt Ruth
(Dad's oldest sister), her husband, Roy, Mom with Gib
hanging over her shoulder, Barbie, our favorite cousin
and her brother Stan. Kneeling is Pete's wife Hazel and
their two kids, Margaret Kilmartin, Gayle,
Margaret Ann Kilmartin and Connie.

Mushroom Medley

In the first edition of this book I included my recipe for Mushroom Ragout which we all loved but after Dave Limp married into the family and served his Mushroom Medley I conceded. His dish is simpler and tastier than mine so why leave mine in the book. Isn't it wonderful to have such a talented son-in-law. While Dave spent many hours perfecting this recipe we only have to follow his directions. You can serve it as a main course or as a side dish. This dish can easily be made ahead of your dinner if you don't have to worry about people raiding your refrigerator and eating this before the planned meal.

This is a great dish and fun to make. Shop at a grocery store that carries many varieties of mushrooms and if you can't find all these, substitute the missing ones with others of your choice.

What you need:

1 pound baby shitake mushrooms

½ pound oyster mushrooms

½ pound tall white button mushrooms (these are the clumpy rooted ones)

3 tablespoons unsalted butter

2 teaspoons cayenne pepper (or less if your don't like picante)

2 teaspoons spice mixture (I use Vegetable Magic from Paul Prudhomme)

4 green onions

2 cloves garlic, chopped

3/4 cup chicken stock

1 ½ tablespoons brandy

Salt and pepper to taste

How to assemble:

Carefully clean and trim the mushrooms and set aside

Melt 1 tablespoon of the butter in a pan

Add the diced green onions (only use the white and white/green part of the onions, not the full green at the ends).

Sauté the onion until they are transparent (2-3 minutes)

Add the cayenne and garlic

Cook for an addition 30 seconds.

Add the mushrooms and stir.

As mushrooms start reducing add the remaining butter.

Cook until mushrooms have softened and released their water (should reduce by more than half)

Add the spice mixture and stir in completely.

Glaze with the Brandy (The Brandy makes the mushrooms shine in more ways than one.)

Stir the mushrooms to cook off the alcohol.

Add the chicken stock.

Simmer until chicken stock has been absorbed.

Salt and pepper to taste and serve.

Serves about 6.

Notes:

Dave often will vary the recipe a little by drizzling some white truffle oil on the mushrooms at the very end. This makes for a much richer dish. For certain main courses it is simply the best.

Pesto Sauce

Have you ever grown basil? Or been tempted to pick up a bunch of the fresh, fragrant herb in the market? Well here's a recipe to make Pesto and make use of that wonderful herb. Use this sauce tossed in hot pasta with a handful of pine nuts or spread it on bread before popping the bread under the broiler. Don't feel you have to use it all, it keeps in the refrigerator for weeks or freeze it for a couple of months.

What you need:

1 cup tightly packed fresh basil leaves
½ cup olive oil
2 tablespoons pine nuts
2 garlic cloves peeled
1/4 teaspoon salt
1/4 cup grated Parmesan or Romano cheese

How to assemble:

Wash, dry and select pretty basil leaves and tightly pack a measuring
   cup
Using a blender or a Cusinart add basil, olive oil, pine nuts, garlic
   and salt
Blend on high speed until pesto is smooth, scraped down the sides
   of the bowl and add the cheese, mix with a short burst
Pour into a small bowl
Refrigerate until use

Notes:

Phyllo Spinach Pie

This makes a nice brunch or lunch dish as well as a side dish for the main meal. Actually I make little hors d'oeuvres out of this instead of a pie. I explain that process in the variations of this recipe.

What you need:

1 cup cottage cheese
1 package frozen chopped spinach (thawed and drained)
3 green onions, chopped
2 cups grated Monterey Jack cheese
1 egg beaten
1 tablespoon lemon juice
½ teaspoon salt
fresh pepper to taste
10 sheets Phyllo dough (buy it in packages in the bread section in the freezer at your market)
1/4 cup melted butter (½ cube)

How to assemble:

In a Cuisinart add the cottage cheese, onions, egg, lemon juice, salt and pepper and mix with short bursts
Add spinach and mix again
Add cheese and finish blending
Set aside to fill pie
Lay Phyllo dough out on a flat surface and cover with a damp towel while working on the pie
Take one sheet and fold in half to form a rectangle
Brush with melted butter

Lay sheet slightly over one half of the pie plate

Repeat this process three times, the next across the other side, then turn place ½ turn and do the next two over the plate going the other way

The bottom of the plate will be covered and the ends will be draping over the edge of the pie plate

Spoon the filling into the pie plate

Fold ends of Phyllo dough over the pie filling, don't worry if it doesn't completely fill the top of the pie

Remove another sheet of Phyllo dough, do not fold, brush with butter and slightly crinkle the dough and arrange it on top of the pie

Repeat this until all sheets have been used

Bake the pie in a pre-heated oven at 350° for about 45 minutes

Dough should be golden brown

Remove and serve

Variations:

Cut Phyllo dough in half

Take one half and fold in half again, brushing with butter

Fold one more time

Spoon a small amount of filling in center and fold ends over making a pocket. Seal the ends with water

Brush top with butter and place on a baking sheet

When all have been arranged on the baking sheet

Bake in a pre-heated oven at 350° for about 20 minutes until pastry is golden brown

Cool slightly before serving as a finger food

Add a pound of crisply fried, crumbled bacon to the filling

Add a pound of cooked, crumbled bulk sausage to the spinach filling

Replace 1 cup of Monterey Jack Cheese with Swiss Cheese in making
the filling

Notes:

Scalloped Potatoes

This was my favorite potato dish as a young girl and I make it once in a while now. I forget how much everyone likes it and every time I make it I vow I'll do it more often, but then I forget again. This is a good dish for a buffet or pot luck.

What you need:

4 lbs baking potatoes
salt and pepper to taste
1 cup of milk
3 tablespoons flour
2 tablespoons butter or margarine
2 tablespoons dried minced onion
½ cup grated Parmasen, Romano or Asiago cheese

How to assemble:

Peel and rinse the potatoes
Slice the potatoes thin

Use a large rectangular baking dish, spray well with PAM

Spread 1/3 potato slices on the bottom of dish

Sprinkle 1 tablespoon of dried mince onions over the layer of potatoes

Sprinkle with salt and pepper

Sprinkle with 2 tablespoons of cheese

Sprinkle with 1 ½ tablespoons of flour

Dot with 1 tablespoon of butter

Repeat this layer

Final layer spread the last of the potatoes

Pour in milk so it reaches to ½ inch from top of baking dish (add more milk if necessary) but should not cover the top of the potatoes

Sprinkle the remaining grated cheese on top

Bake in a pre-heated oven at 350° for about 1 hour,

Remove from oven and test for tenderness of the potatoes by jabbing with a fork

If not done, bake another 20 minutes

Cool about 10 minutes

Serve

Variations:

Layer sliced ham and double the cheese to turn this into a main dish for a meal.

Notes:

Turkey/Oyster Stuffing

When Dave and I had our first Thanksgiving together we were both nervous about making sure that everyone's traditions were protected. Our combined family was present plus my parents. We had several discussions about the stuffing and finally decided to make three, cornbread, traditional bread, and oyster stuffing, which was my mother's favorite. When all was done and eaten we discovered a whole new group of fans for oyster stuffing and no one could tell the difference between the cornbread stuffing and the traditional. So from then on we make two stuffings and everyone is happy.

We usually make our stuffing the night before but we must caution you never to stuff the turkey until just before putting it in the oven. Also don't forget to remove all the stuffing before refrigerating the leftover turkey to prevent any possibility of food poisoning.

But now Dave and I make the stuffing the night before and then bake it in the oven with the turkey neck on top while roasting the turkey on the barbeque. That works very well for our family because we've been getting a 30 + pound bird and stuffing it alters the cooking time too much. The following recipe is for cornbread or traditional stuffing, changes for oyster stuffing are in italics.

What you need:

Unseasoned cornbread or bread stuffing mix for 15 lb turkey

2 medium onions, peeled and chopped finely
4 stalks of celery, including leaves, cleaned and chopped fine
3-4 green onions, chopped fine
2 eggs beaten
1 or 2 cans of chicken broth
1/4 cup fresh parsley chopped fine
1 teaspoon salt
½ teaspoon white or black pepper
1 tablespoon poultry seasoning (add to taste)
2 jars fresh shucked oysters (buy from your meat market)
1 large turkey neck or 2 small necks or 1 large turkey tail

How to assemble:

In a very large bowl pour in the dried crumbs
Add the chopped vegetables
Sprinkle the salt, pepper and poultry seasoning on the mix
Add the beaten eggs and mix well
Add oysters and juice (if oysters are large cut them in two)
Add the chicken broth to moisten (Remember it takes a while for
    the dried crumbs to absorb the moisture so add a little more
    than you think is the right amount.)
Let sit for about 20 minutes
Stir stuffing again, add more broth if needed, and more seasoning
    or salt if desired
At this point the stuffing can be chilled until time to cook

Baking Variations:

Stuffing Turkey:
Just before baking the turkey dry out the cavity with a paper towel
Spoon in stuffing, filling cavity to only about 2/3 full to allow the
    stuffing to expend while baking
Turn turkey over and spoon more stuffing in neck cavity, pull skin
    over the opening and secure it with a metal scewer.

In the oven:
Spoon stuffing into a greased baking dish, lay turkey neck or tail
on top and cover the dish with foil

1 ½ hours prior to serving dinner put the dish in the oven
Bake covered for 45 minutes in an oven pre-heated to 350°
Uncover the dish and bake for 30 to 45 minutes to finish

Notes:

And yet another Thanksgiving, apparently one of the few days we remember to take pictures. Here is Gage, Marc and Rocelle's son, Nicole, Amy, Janet, Danielle and Sherrill.

Yorkshire Pudding

I never made this until I became a Wigglesworth. In fact, I had never tasted it. It took a while to find the recipe, one that Grandma Janet pronounced was right. Don't be fooled by those fancy puffy things, more like a cream puff pastry, this eggy pudding that collapses minutes after coming out of the oven is the real thing.

The first few times I made this I was a nervous wreck trying to get everything done in time and on the table. Since then I've learned a few tricks that made it easy. This dish is traditionally served with roast beef or lamb but I've found that it also goes well with pot roast. If there is any left at the end of the meal, the people in my family eat it cold before going home. But then maybe we're different. You know they are part Yorkshiremen.

What you need:

Serves 6 to 12 depending on how much they like it.

1 ½ cups flour
6 medium eggs (if jumbo eggs, use 5)
2 teaspoons salt
1 ½ cups milk

How to assemble:

Combine all ingredients and beat until smooth
The batter should be the consistency of cream, if too thick add a
  little water
Refrigerate at least 2 hours before cooking

Baking:

Use a large shallow baking or roasting pan. Remember, this pan will be placed on the table to serve from

Spray with PAM

Add dripping from the roasting pan if you are serving roasted meat (if you have no dripping make some by dissolving 1 beef bullion cube in 1/4 cup hot water, plus 2 tablespoon of olive oil.)

Heat the pan and drippings for a few minutes in a pre-heated oven at 400°

Add batter to pan. Batter shouldn't be more than an inch or so in the bottom of the pan and make sure the oven rack is down in the bottom part of the oven to leave lots of room for the pudding to rise.

Close the oven door and set a time for 20 minutes

Do not open the oven door.

When the timer sounds, remove the pudding and set on the table.

It is somewhat dramatic if you can get everyone seated before the pudding is put on the table. Everyone will ooh and aah and then the pudding will deflate. But worry not, it still tastes good.

Don't even think of transferring it to a serving dish, what it's baked in is what it's served in.

Traditionally, gravy or au jus is poured over a piece of this on the plate.

Notes:

Main Courses

*Mom and Dad, in the 1950's. They taught me to cook
and how fun it was to be a gracious hostess.*

CONTENTS

Aunt Nell's Pork Chops

When I was a teenager I would visit Aunt Nell, my mother's oldest sister, during the summer. While these visits started with Connie and I both going, as we got older she would have a summer job so I went by myself. Aunt Nell worked in a fabric store during this time and became quite a seamstress so during my visits she taught me to sew. But she was also a very good cook and as she only cooked for two, her cooking was very different from what I knew. This was one of her dinners that was a favorite of mine. Our family rarely had chops or steaks because we never knew how many drop in's we would have at dinner time and it's hard to serve a half of pork chop without the guest noticing. So I didn't have the opportunity to recreate this dish until I moved to San Francisco and cooked for my roommates. I think it's a yummy way to serve pork chops.

What you need:

4-6 pork chops (2 per person)
1 tablespoon oil
1 large onion
1 large tomato (beefsteak if possible)
1 box frozen peas
1/4 cup white wine
1 teaspoon salt
fresh pepper to taste

How to assemble:

In a large skillet heat oil
Salt and pepper the pork chops

Lay the pork chops in the hot skillet and brown one side
Turn the pork chops over and brown the second side
Peel and slice the onion (slice 1/4 inch thick)
Put a slice of onion on each pork chop
Put a slice of tomato on top of the onion on each pork chop
Pour the frozen peas over all the pork chops
Add the wine
Cover the skillet and simmer until done (about 20 minutes)
Dish up each chop with the onion and tomato slices on top
Scoop up the peas and juice and pour over the chop on the serving
    plate

Notes:

This dish goes very well with mashed potatoes

Barbeque Ribs

I loved barbeque ribs but didn't have a clue about how to make them. That didn't stop me. I experimented and served them at least three different times to dismayed guests who gamely tried to flake off the charred outer layer looking for something edible underneath. I was beginning to run out of willing guests and still wasn't close to having a success.

Finally, one of the guys at work, who was always bragging about the big barbeques at his house, took pity on me. Or, maybe he just got tired of my whining. Anyway he shared his secret recipe with me and you've all sampled that success. I never have trouble getting people to come over for barbeque ribs these days.

Danielle used to frequently select these for her birthday dinner and the year Dave and I got married she wanted ribs. We had a houseful with my sister, Teresa and Ken and their kids with us for the week, plus my friend, Vanya's daughter was visiting. And in addition to the usual Sunday dinner crowd Dave's brother and his wife were joining us. So I carefully calculated the pounds of ribs I would need and added a little for good measure. Dave went out to buy the 15 pounds of ribs. Well, he automatically doubled it to make sure there would be enough. It seemed that I cooked for days. But actually it worked out because we made a large dent in them at that dinner and then all the house guests gorged themselves for the rest of their visit and we didn't have to cook again. Since that time we have worked out our estimates so we get closer to the needed amount but we still usually buy much more that we need, always fearful the dreaded, "not enough food" situation will arise.

What you need:

4-5 lbs of pork spareribs (Usually ½ lb per person for spareribs
and less if using country style)
Salt
Garlic granules
Pepper
Lowry's Unseasoned Meat Tenderizer

Sauce:
3 cups of your favorite barbeque sauce *plus:*
½ cup molasses
2 tablespoons Lea & Perins Worcestershire Sauce
2 teaspoons dry mustard
2 tablespoons vinegar or lemon juice
Juice from 1 medium onion, grated finely, throw away the pressed
pulp
Catsup to taste

How to assemble:

Preparing Ribs:
Rinse ribs the night before and pat dry
Sprinkle ribs with garlic granules, salt, pepper and tenderizer
Poke meat with fork to allow condiments to absorb
Turn ribs over and repeat process
Cover tightly and refrigerate over night or at least for 5 hours.

Cooking ribs:
Roast ribs on a rack, in a roasting pan, in the oven at 350° for
about 1 hour or until ribs are brown and the meat is tender
and coming away from the bones. or
Cook ribs on barbeque grill about 30-40 minutes until ribs are
brown and the meat is tender and coming away from the bones.
Cool the ribs slightly and cut into serving size slabs (usually two
to three ribs)

Preparing sauce:

Assemble all the ingredients in a large sauce pan and bring to a
boil

Taste the sauce, it should be sweet and slightly pungent with a
small bite.

Adjust the flavor as needed by adding a little of each ingredient
until you reach the combination that pleases you. Remember
that each time you make this sauce it will be a little different
but basically the same.

Finishing ribs:

Dip each slab into the hot sauce and lay it in a baking pan

Cover the pan tightly with foil

Bake in a pre-heated oven at 300° for thirty minutes

Serve

Alternative finishing method:

Marc and Rocelle paint their cooked ribs with sauce and lay them
on the barbeque grill for five minutes, turn them over and
paint and grill the other side. If you are using this method,
don't cut the ribs apart until after this process, just before
serving.

Notes:

If you like your barbeque sauce with a little bite to it, carefully
add just a tiny bit of cayenne pepper, increasing it slowly because
a little goes a long way.

Use this sauce to finish off your chicken too.

Beef Stew and Dumplings

This is a great dish, the fragrance is soothing while the meal is hearty and economical. I cooked this many times before I had Danielle and it always reminds me of cold rainy Saturdays with the pleasant anticipation of friends for the evening.

This is an entire meal so serve it with a green salad or fruit and you've covered your basic food groups.

What you need:

Stew:
2 lbs of stewing beef
2 tablespoons oil
1 ½ cups of red table wine
1 ½ cups of beef broth
1 teaspoon salt (or to taste)
1 teaspoon pepper (or to taste)
1 tablespoon Beau Monde (spice mix)
½ teaspoon thyme
1/8 teaspoon rosemary
1 teaspoon garlic granules
2 cups of sliced carrots
4 medium onions, peeled and quartered
1 cup sliced green bell peppers

Dumplings:
2 cups Bisquick
3/4 cup milk
½ teaspoon Beau Monde

How to assemble:

Stew:

Brown beef in hot oil in a large heavy pot

While the meat is browning combine wine, broth, herbs, salt and pepper and let set for five minutes

When meat is thoroughly browned on all sides use a portion of the liquid to deglaze the pan (put about a 1/4 cup of liquid in the hot pan and let it boil up all the goodness and brown pieces stuck to the bottom and sides)

Stir until all bits of brown are released and in the broth

Add the rest of the liquid mixture

Reduce fire to low

Cover pot and simmer for 1-2 hours

Add vegetables and simmer ½ hour

Dumplings:

Combine Beau Monde, Bisquick and milk

Dough should be sticky

Uncover pot and move meat to the center, leaving space around the sides for the dumplings

Increase the heat so the broth is boiling

Drop small spoonfuls of dough into the broth (dough should be about 1 ½ inch diameter)

Let boil for 10 minutes

Cover pot and reduce heat to low

Simmer for 15 minutes

Serve

Hint: If you have more dough than the pot will hold discard it or drop it in spoonfuls on a greased cookie sheet and bake it in the oven at 350° for 30-45 minutes.

Notes:

Beef Stroganoff

This was one of my special dishes. For years I made it from scratch until I learned how well it worked with any leftover beef. When Danielle and I lived in San Francisco, we used to serve an elegant Christmas dinner for our extended "family." The meal consisted of roast beef, baked potatoes, sour cream, sauteed mushrooms, the works. One year on the day after Christmas my cousin, Fred Watson, and his wife, Sherry, were in the neighborhood and came by to visit. Of course when the visit crept into the dinner hour I invited them to stay for leftovers. I whipped into the kitchen knowing I had served a dinner with all the ingredients for this dish the day before and in the time it took to boil the rice had this meal on the table. They were gratifyingly astounded, and I admit to being a little smug.

What you need:

serves 8-10
2 lbs of lean steak, cubed
2 tablespoon olive oil
2 envelopes of Lipton's Dried Onion Soup
2 cans of Campbell's Cream of Mushroom Soup
1 lb of fresh mushroom, cleaned and sliced
1 pint of sour cream
2 cups of rice
4 cups of water

How to assemble:

In a heavy pot brown the steak in the olive oil

Add the onion soup mix, lower heat, cover and cook about 20 minutes

Add the mushrooms and the two cans of mushroom soup (do not dilute the soup)

Cover and cook about 15 minutes, stirring occasionally, then turn heat to low until ready to serve.

Meanwhile, bring the rice to a boil in the water in an uncovered pan.

Boil until the water falls below the level of rice and craters form

Cover pot tightly, turn fire to low, cook 25 minutes.

Five minutes before serving, remove beef mixture from burner so mixture is not bubbling.

Add sour cream, stir well and serve with rice.

Notes:

If you plan to use leftover roast beef in this recipe do the following:

Cube the beef, cutting out and discarding any fat.

Put the cubed meat along with the juices from the platter and freeze until using.

Start the recipe at the onion soup, add the defrosted beef and juices and follow the recipe.

Black Bean Chili

This is a recipe I made up from good things I've tried, so naturally I love it. I won second place in a chili contest at work with this but the grand prize is the winter day I served it for Sunday dinner. There wasn't enough left to freeze for another day. By the way, this is one of those dishes it makes sense to cook extra and freeze some for another dinner.

What you need:

large, heavy cooking pot, sprayed with PAM
2 to 3 lbs pork roast
2 to 3 lbs chuck roast
2 to 3 lbs black beans
2 or 3 large brown onions
2 tablespoons olive oil
2 to 3 oz. Schilling or Gebhart Chili Powder
2 tablespoons ground cumin
1 teaspoon salt
meat stock from roasts, defatted
2 cups beef bouillon or 2 prepared Au Jus Mix packets

Advanced Preparation:

Sprinkle the chuck and pork roasts with salt, pepper and garlic granules
Brown roasts in deep kettle in 2 tablespoons of olive oil, making sure all
    sides are deep brown (Note: you may have to brown them one or
    two at a time and then when complete return them all to the pot)
Add 1/4 or 1/2 cup of water to deglaze the pot used for browning
Simmer the meat 3 or 4 hours until very tender (note: add more water
    if necessary but usually the meat will generate sufficient broth)

When done remove meat and cool.

Remove all fat and bones from roast and shred meat, refrigerate overnight or a couple of days until you assemble the chili.

Pour broth in container and refrigerate.

Next day remove all congealed fat from chilled broth and keep until you assemble chili. (Note: You can freeze meat and broth at this point to assemble at a later date)

The day before assembling chili soak beans in cool water overnight.

How to assemble:

Coarsely chop onion and brown in deep pot in olive oil.

Add broth from roasts (Meat Stock)

Add meat

Rinse and drain beans and add to pot

Add bouillon or Au Jus Mix and appropriate water

Add chili powder (maybe 1/2 bottle to start) Add later to taste

Add 1 teaspoon of salt (adjust to taste later)

Add cumin

Simmer 2 to 3 hours or until beans are tender.

Be sure to taste and add chili powder, cumin, salt and water to meet your taste. (If you like it hot carefully add some cayenne pepper for zip, too much will ruin the chili)

Suggestions for Serving:

Top with sour cream and fresh cilantro, or cheese and raw onions

Serve with wedges of tortillas to make this a great meal.

Or make your own tortillas.

Freezes well.

Notes:

Black Beans and Pork

Dave met and married his first wife, Rita, in Mexico City where they both lived for several years. She was from New York City but had family roots from the Yucatan. This is just one of several dishes that were passed down from her side of the family. When we serve this dish it becomes a family affair because we have to have homemade tortillas to make it perfect. Everyone helps in pressing and cooking the tortillas. But it's worth the effort. This is one of my favorites, and one I used to request for my Birthday dinner. Dave always cooks it, I just enjoy eating it.

What you need:

2-3 lbs pork shoulder or picnic roast
2-3 lbs black beans
2 medium onions, chopped
1 teaspoon garlic granules
1 teaspoon salt
1 teaspoon pepper
2 tablespoons Epazote powder

How to assemble:

Carefully pick through the beans removing any stones or damaged beans.
Cover the beans with cold water and let set over night
Remove fat and bones from pork
Cube the meat
Using a piece of the pork fat, render it down in a large pot and then brown the cubed pork

Add the onions and cook until soft
Remove any pork fat still in the pan
Rinse and drain the beans
Add the beans to the pork
Throw in any pork bones, discarding all the fat at this point
Add the seasonings
Add enough water to cover the beans and the meat
Simmer for 3-4 hours, until beans are tender
Add water as needed
Skim off fat on surface
Remove bones, pull off any meat adhered to the bones and put the
    meat back in the pot, discarding the bones.
Serve with sour cream and chopped onions
Some of the kids like to add hot pepper sauce

Notes:

You may find it helpful to find a Mexican Grocery store in your area to buy the Epazote and also use as a source for the corn flour. Or if you want you might want to even buy fresh tortillas.

Brett's Jerked Pork Chops

Before Janet and Brett got married, they ate out most evenings, which in the heart of San Francisco is easy and tempting to do. But it is expensive. So with marriage and responsibilities came the decision to start cooking family dinners. Brett discovered this dish and they've been enjoying it as well as many other home cooked meals, ever since. The quick prep time and delicious flavors make it a big weeknight hit.

What you need:

2 teaspoons onion power
1 teaspoon sugar
1 teaspoon dried thyme leaves
½ teaspoon salt
½ teaspoon ground allspice
½ teaspoon ground red pepper
¼ teaspoon ground nutmeg
4 boneless pork loin chops
4 cups cooked white rice
2 green onions, finely chopped

How to assemble:

Combine spices (first 7 ingredients) and mix well.
Rub spice mixture on to both sides of the pork chops
Spray a nonstick skillet with PAM
Heat skillet over medium heat

Cook pork chops about 5 minutes per side or until juicy and barely
    pink in center. Serve pork chops over rice
Garnish with a sprinkle of chopped green onions

Hints:

You can make a large batch of the spice to have on hand. Just seal it in an airtight container. Also you should adjust the red pepper to the level of picante (hot) your family perfers.

Notes:

Janet and her husband, Brett Hancock
He does most of the cooking at their house.

Chicken and Rice Bake

Granny first served us this when Danielle and I went to visit them one weekend in Lompoc. They lived in that beautiful little town for about two years but it was too far from all the family. Poppa loved it because of the flower fields and the broken down barns that made such good subjects for his painting but Granny was just too lonely without all her family and friends. We finally talked them into moving back to Long Beach. Linda found them a darling place. On a Friday they took a suitcase and went to Connie's for the weekend, meanwhile all of us kids went to Lompoc and packed them up, moved them out and installed them in their new apartment so that Sunday night they were in their new place. Painless for them. And in subsequent years it proved to be worth the trouble to have them back, close to the rest of the family and all their old friends.

What you need:

2-3 lbs of chicken pieces
1 can cream of mushroom soup
½ cup water
3/4 cup orange juice
½ cup white wine
1 package Lipton Onion soup mix
1 cup long grain white rice, uncooked

How to assemble:

Mix mushroom soup, water, orange juice and wine in a bowl
Grease a 13 x 9 baking dish
Sprinkle rice evenly over the bottom of the baking dish
Dip each piece of chicken in the liquid in the bowl and lay chicken
    on the rice
Pour the remaining liquid over the chicken and rice
Sprinkle the onion soup mix over top of the dish
Cover the dish tightly with foil
Bake in a pre-heated oven at 325° for 2 ½ hours

Notes:

Chicken Florentine

Margaret worked with me at Wells Fargo Bank where she was our chief social guru. I'm sure you've seen other recipes she's provided me in this book (especially check out her Bourbon Balls). I could probably fill a book with her recipes alone.

Anyway, after we finished our big project in the early 80's several of us stayed in touch, getting together for lunches and dinners a few times a year. This is one of the dishes she served us at a luncheon at her apartment on Russian Hill. I liked it so much that I subsequently made it for Sunday dinners.

What you need:

1 ½ pound of fresh spinach leaves or 2 10oz packages of frozen spinach, thawed
2 teaspoons lemon juice
½ teaspoon salt
1/8 teaspoon pepper
2 ½ cups of cooked, diced chicken
2 large cans of White Sauce
1 tablespoon of chicken stock base (dried powder or three smashed bouillon cubes
2 tablespoons dry Sherry
1/4 cup grated Parmesan cheese
dash of paprika

How to assemble:

Spread the spinach over the bottom of a greased baking dish
Sprinkle with lemon juice

Spread the cubed chicken evenly over the spinach

Sprinkle with salt and pepper

In a separate bowl combine the white sauce, the chicken stock base and the sherry

Mix well and pour over the chicken and spinach

Sprinkle the cheese over the top

Add a few dashes of paprika to give the dish some color

Bake in a pre-heated oven at 350° for 30 minutes

Serve with rice or noodles

Serves about 6

Notes:

Chicken Kung Pao

I went through a long Chinese period, mostly while we were in the Goldhunter house where we entertained a lot. That house was in Foster City on the water and we lived there when we visited China, and we attended some of the classes put on at the school run by Martin Yan of "Yan Can Cook". So no wonder I went through my Chinese period. My favorite was Szechuan dishes until Dave finally begged for mercy. I guess my growing addiction to red peppers finally got to him. This is one of the recipes I actually followed but mostly I experimented. I would start with crushed and chopped garlic sauteed with chopped red peppers and fresh ginger until the steam brought tears to my eyes, then I added some kind of meat or fish, some kind of vegetable and some sauce from any Chinese bottle. It was always good and oh how it cleared those sinuses. You can try that or this recipe.

What you need:

1 lb skinless, boneless, cubed chicken
8 small dried red peppers
½ cup roasted, unsalted peanuts
1 teaspoon peeled, chopped fresh ginger
1 tablespoon soy sauce
1 ½ tablespoon cornstarch
2-3 tablespoon oil

Sauce:
2 tablespoons soy sauce
1 tablespoon white wine
1 tablespoon sugar

½ tablespoon cider vinegar
1 teaspoon cornstarch
½ teaspoon salt
1 teaspoon sesame oil

How to assemble:

Mix soy sauce and cornstarch and soak with cubed chicken for 30
   minutes
Meanwhile clean red peppers and remove all seeds
Cut red peppers into slivers and set aside
Peel and chop ginger and set aside
Assemble all the ingredients for the sauce in a separate bowl
In a wok or heavy fry pan heat the oil to about 300° and quickly
   stir fry the cubed chicken
Remove the chicken to a plate covered with paper towel to drain
Pour out oil and replace with fresh oil
Fry pepper slivers until they turn black,
Add ginger and chicken, stirring quickly
Stir in ingredients for sauce and bring to boil
Stir constantly until sauce is thickened
Take off the fire, add peanuts and serve immediately

Hint:

This recipe works equally well with pork replacing chicken.

Notes:

If you're afraid of peppers, use only two to start.

Chicken Fettuccini

This is a variation of my Clam Fettuccini for those who do not like clams or those of you that have leftover chicken to use up. It's easy and nutritious. You can always make the sauce either a day or a couple of hours ahead but make sure that you heat it on top of the stove without bringing it to a boil or you're liable to change the consistency of the sauce. This is an extremely easy and tasty meal.

What you need:

1 pkg fresh pasta from the deli section of the super market. (I suggest fettuccini or tortellini or both and mix them.)
2 halves of chicken breast
1 cup low fat sour cream
4-5 cloves of fresh garlic
½ cup grated cheese such as Parmesan or Asiago salt and pepper to taste
½ teaspoon of parsley

How to assemble:

Poach the chicken breasts in 1/4 cup of water or chicken broth. Skin and bone the meat, cut into bite size pieces and cool.
Strain the broth to make 1 cup. (You can increase broth using hot water and a chicken bullion cube if necessary)
Smash the garlic cloves, chop finely and fry in 1 tablespoon of butter until toasty brown.
When the garlic is just right add the chicken broth and continue cooking until the mixture is reduced to one quarter of the original amount. Add the chicken at this point, then remove

the mixture from the flames. When the mixture is no longer bubbling, add the sour cream and stir.

Meanwhile prepare pasta according to the directions on the package and then drain.

Put the pasta in a large shallow serving bowl, sprinkle it with ½ cup of cheese, pour on the sauce and the parsley then toss. Serves 2-3.

Notes:

Cioppino

Cioppino is the ultimate San Francisco dish to be served with plenty of sour dough bread. This is a delightful fish stew in a spicy tomato broth and there are no rules about what it has to contain. When I decide to serve this I first check out the local fish market to see what is available. Remember that this is a dish the guests have to get into so don't serve it at an elegant evening. Its more for your best friends, casually dressed who are into good food, wine and conversation. Then if people get the sauce all over themselves and the tablecloth, who cares?

What you need:

½ lb each of 2 different fish, boned and cubed
1 lb prawns, shelled and deveined
½ lb of calamari (optional)
2 cans minced or chopped clams, drained (retain liquid)
1 dozen mussels
2 dozen assorted clams
1 Dungeness crab, cooked and cleaned but still in the shell

Sauce:
5-6 cups of Gayle's Marinara Sauce (see this book) or
1 large onion chopped fine
1 large bell pepper seeded and chopped fine
4 cloves of garlic, smashed and chopped
2 tablespoons of olive oil
1 tablespoon Italian Spice
½ teaspoon salt
1 15 oz can tomato puree

1 8 oz can tomato sauce and
Clam juice from drained cans
1 cup white wine
1/4 teaspoon cayenne pepper
½ teaspoon garlic granules

How to assemble:

In a large pot saute the onions, pepper and garlic until tender
Add tomato sauce and puree and bring to a boil
Add the Italian seasoning and salt
Let simmer for ½ hour or
Pour Gayle's Marinara Sauce into a large pot
In both cases continue with sauce as follows:
Add clam juice from cans of drained clams
Add garlic granules, cayenne pepper and white wine
Let simmer uncovered for ½ to 1 hour
Meanwhile assemble fish and wash and clean mussels and clams
Approximately ½ hour before serving time add uncooked fish to
    sauce, except for mussels and clams
Continue to simmer for 20 minutes
Add cooked fish, (crab and etc.) and mussels and clam
Cover and simmer for 10 minutes
Serve immediately in large shallow bowls

Hint: If you have leftovers of this dish, it is better to shell the fish
    and refrigerate only the fish meat and sauce to be heated up
    another time. I would not recommend freezing this dish as all
    fish have different freezer life spans. Remember my rule, *if you
    can buy it in the freezer section of the market you can freeze it.* Ever
    seen this dish in the freezer section?

Notes:

Crab Cakes

Dave and I love crab cakes and when we went to the Macy's Chefs' Tour, our chef, Nancy Oakes (from the Boulevard), made them for us. It was our lucky day. These crab cakes were exceptional and Nancy took the mystery out of making them. But I must caution you, you need to use fresh tasty crab, don't skimp on this. I've served these as a starter to a nice dinner and as the main course, either way they are memorable.

What you need:

1 lb fresh crab meat (usually about 2 medium Dungeness crabs shelled)
2 cups of fresh bread crumbs
2 tablespoons olive oil
2/3 cup celery, finely chopped
½ cup red onion, finely chopped
1 ½ teaspoon Worcestershire sauce
1/4 cup parsley, finely chopped
2 tablespoons thyme, finely chopped
1 tablespoon Dijon mustard
1 teaspoon Tabasco sauce
½ teaspoon red pepper flakes
3 eggs separated
salt and pepper to taste

How to assemble:

Use a good sweet french bread, day old, and remove crusts. Cut with a knife into crumbs approximately the size of peas. Toss in the olive oil and let set at least one hour before using.

Meanwhile chop the vegetables and put in large mixing bowl

Add all the ingredients, including the bread crumbs, but excluding the eggs

Toss lightly so all ingredients are mixed

Separate the eggs

Add the yolks to the crab mixture and stir well

Whip the egg whites to stiff peaks

Fold whites into the crab mixture

Form mixture into 3 inch balls

Place crab cakes in hot saute pan lightly filmed with oil

Brown on one side, flip and brown on the other side

Remove to baking sheet

The above steps can be completed up to a couple of hours before serving

20 minutes before serving, place the baking sheet in a 350° oven.

Serve on a bed of greens with a spoon full of tartar sauce.

I served two to each of my six guests and had leftovers for the next day.

Notes:

This dish is only as good as the main ingredient so make sure your crab is tasty.

Dave's Meatloaf

Some dishes are impossible to do well in small quantities. I think meatloaf is one of them. So rather than try to cook meatloaf for Danielle and I, I relied on one of my friends to invite me to dinner when she planned to make it. You can imagine my delight when shortly after our marriage I found that meatloaf was one of Dave's specialities.

Danielle and I looked forward to that first meatloaf. Danielle had invited a new friend over and most of the older kids were there. Dave proudly served the meatloaf and we stared in horror at the two yellow eyes glaring at us out of each slice. We didn't know, and probably didn't appreciate, that he stuffed the meat loaf with boiled eggs for effect. When we got past that shock, I excused myself to go get the catsup. I returned to find Dave open-mouthed and the kids quivering with nervousness. I learned Dave considered it an insult to his meatloaf to use catsup. Luckily, he was still very smitten, and the marriage survived. I could not compromise on this, I have to have catsup with meatloaf. And the kids were more than happy that I broke through that barrier.

I still like meatloaf. I love Dave's meatloaf, but now he rarely stuffs it with boiled eggs and doesn't get hurt when the catsup is used, as long as he doesn't have to use it himself.

What you need:

1 lb ground pork
1 lb ground beef
1 lb ground veal
3 eggs, beaten
½ cup of fine bread crumbs

1 medium onion, grated
1 teaspoon salt
½ teaspoon pepper

How to assemble:

Mix the 3 types of ground meat together (Some meat markets will
   grind them together for you if you ask)
Add the egg, bread crumbs, onion and seasonings and using your
   hands mix together thoroughly.
Form the meat into a loaf and lay it in a baking pan or place it in
   a large loaf pan
Bake in a pre-heated 325° oven for approximately 1 hour
Remove meatloaf to plate and serve.

Variations:

Add 2 tablespoons of Worchershire Sauce to meat mixture before
   baking.
Form bottom half of loaf and lay 6 peeled, hard boiled eggs on
   top, then add the rest of the meat to form a loaf.
Form bottom half of loaf and lay large mushroom caps on top,
   then add the rest of the meat to form a loaf.
Lay 3 slices of bacon on top of the meatloaf before baking.

Notes:

Fettuccini a la Gayle

I saw Jill St. John make something similar to this dish many years ago on a talk show. It was so simple and turned out so delicious that I've been making my own version since. Don't be afraid to experiment, it's hard to go wrong. I usually have the ingredients for this dish on hand.

What You need:

1 pkg fresh pasta from the deli section of the super market. (*I usually use fettuccini but it works equally well with Angel Hair or even Tortellini. Or mix your favorites.*)
1 small can of chopped clams. 6 ½ ozs.
1 cup low fat sour cream
4-5 cloves of fresh garlic
1 tablespoon butter or olive oil
½ cup grated cheese such as Parmesan or Asiago
salt and pepper to taste
1 lb. various seafood cut in small pieces

How to assemble:

Smash the garlic cloves, chop finely and fry in butter or oil until toasty brown.

Meanwhile open the can of chopped clams and drain the juice. When the garlic is just right add the clam juice and continue cooking until the mixture is reduced to one half.

This is the right time to prepare pasta according to the directions on the package and then drain.

If you are adding uncooked fish to the sauce, add it now and cook it until done.

If you are adding cooked shrimp, clams, crab or etc. do it now, then remove the mixture from the flames.

When the mixture is no longer bubbling, add the sour cream and stir. Set aside until serving.

Put the drained pasta in a large shallow serving bowl, sprinkle it with the cheese, pour on the sauce and then toss. Serves 2-3.

If you don't like fish see the variation with Chicken.

Notes:

Fried Chicken

This is how I learned to fry chicken from my mother, the farm girl. Using this method you can produce chicken that competes with the Colonel or Knott's Berry Farm. When we fried chicken it was always plural. My mother bought fresh chickens at a little market near us and for our family of seven she would always buy three. That guaranteed that we all got the piece we wanted no matter how many people stopped by and stayed to dinner.

In those days you didn't just go out and buy pieces, you got the whole thing. You were lucky if they were dressed, meaning the innards were already cleaned out. I never learned to do that but I watched my mother do it many times. But I did learn to cut the chickens up and soak the pieces in salt water before cooking them. I don't know why we used the salt water but recently "brining" has become very popular and the cooks say it is because the salt makes the meat more tender. So the old ways are proven to be right again.

What you need:

2 or 3 lb chicken cut into legs, thighs, wings, ½ breasts (2), and
    back or selected chicken parts weighing the same
2 tablespoon salt water to cover chicken
1 ½ cups flour
2 teaspoons Spice Island Fine Herbs
1 teaspoon celery salt
½ teaspoon garlic granules
1 ½ tablespoon dried onion, mashed to granules
½ teaspoon pepper

1 teaspoon paprika
1 tablespoon Parsley Patch or Salad Seasoning
Cooking oil as needed

How to assemble:

Soak chicken in salt water for several hours or over night. If chicken
is frozen let it thaw in the salt water.
Rinse carefully to remove all the salt and pat dry with a paper towel
Assemble the flour and seasoning in a plastic freezer bag
Heat ½ inch of oil in a heavy skillet
Test for right temperature by flicking a drop of water in the oil, if
it sizzles and snaps its ready for the chicken
Taking the largest pieces first put 4-5 pieces of chicken in the bag
and shake well until the pieces are coated with flour mixture
Lay each piece in the skillet and cook until browned
Turn the pieces until all sides are browned
Take browned pieces and lay them on a rack sitting in a ½ inch
deep baking sheet
Put the baking sheet in the oven, pre-heated to 350°
Continue flouring and frying the chicken until all pieces are
browned and in the oven.
Replenish oil in the skillet as necessary.
The last pieces should be the smallest such as the wings and/or backs
Cook in the oven for another 15 or 20 minutes
This allows the oil on the chicken to drip into the baking sheet
while the chicken finishes cooking.

Variations:

Does your family like it crispy? No problem.
Dredge the chicken pieces in plain flour
Then in beaten eggs

Then shake in flour mixture above
Cook the same way

Notes:

Gayle's Jambalaya Rice

I was making this dish long before I moved to Cajun country and I made it up to suit my family's taste. In many ways its similar to making a Paella but it has an entirely different taste. This is another one dish meal, needing only a salad to round the meal out. You can vary the meat and fish according to what's in the refrigerator, the market or your tastes. And this dish should be picante (hot) but adjusted to your taste.

What you need:

1 lb lean boneless pork (cubed) (Leftover ham or pork will work)
2 ½ lbs chicken drumettes or 1 lb boneless, skinless chicken breast (cubed) or
2 lbs fish fillets, deboned and cubed (Cod or red snapper is good)
1 ½ lbs. jumbo shrimp, shelled and deveined
2 dozen assorted mussels and clams
½ lb hot Italian sausage
2-3 tablespoons olive oil
1 large red bell pepper, deseeded and chopped
2 large onions, chopped
2 cloves of garlic minced
2 cups long grained white rice (uncooked)
4 cups of chicken broth
1 medium can stewed chopped tomatoes or equivalent of homemade marinara sauce (see recipe this book)
1 teaspoon salt
1/8 teaspoon cayenne pepper

How to assemble:

In a large, heavy skillet brown the pork and chicken in the olive oil then remove from the pan. It is not necessary to brown the fish

Crumble the sausage in the skillet and saute with the onions, garlic and peppers (If the sausage is in casings remove the casings before cooking)

Drain the grease from the skillet

The above steps can be done several hours prior to completion of the dish, then.

Stir the rice into the sausage mixture and cook until rice looks opaque.

Stir in the chicken broth, the salt and pepper, and tomatoes

Add the pork and chicken or fish

Bring to boil and let cook uncovered for 20 minutes

Add shrimp

Cover skillet and reduce fire to low

Cook for 30-40 minutes or until the rice is tender

Add mussels and clams

Cover and cook for 10 minutes more

Remove dish from heat and let set for 10 minutes so all juices are absorbed

Put skillet directly on the table and remove lid.

Listen to the oohs and aahs.

Hints:

I frequently make this in a roasting pan and after the rice boils for 20 minute I cover the roaster and put it in the oven to finish cooking. Using that method cook at 350° for 45 minutes before adding the shellfish.

Notes:

Gayle's Mac and Cheese

If your family and friends think Macaroni and Cheese comes out of the box, they're in for a surprise. I made this so many times in my younger years that I guess I had stopped making it by the time I joined the Wigglesworth family. Anyway, one day one of us ordered it at a rather posh local restaurant and everyone raved about it, so I've been making it at home ever since.

This is the dish I always provided for the big pot lucks we had at EurekaBank. I would have liked to bring some other dishes but it was made clear that I would have to bring other dishes plus this one so I gave up.

Never make just one batch, always make extra for the freezer. Take it from the freezer anytime, put it in a cold oven, add a little milk, and bake for twice as long as the recipe calls for.

What you need:

1 pound elbow macaroni boiled 20 minutes until tender, then drained (Add salt and little oil to the water before boiling)

1 pound of your favorite cheese, approximately 3 cups grated (Dave's favorite is Vermont Cheddar but feel free to mix cheeses with compatible flavors. Read *About Cheese* for more information.)

2 cups low fat sour cream

1/4 cup dried onion flakes

½ cup skim milk (approximate)

1 teaspoon salt

1 teaspoon coarsely ground pepper

How to assemble:

While the macaroni is boiling, grate the cheese
In a large bowl mix the sour cream, milk, cheese, onion and salt
  and pepper.
When macaroni is drained, add it to the cheese mixture and stir
  well. (If mixture is dry add more milk)
Pour into baking containers, pre sprayed with PAM.
Bake at 350° for 45 to 60 minutes, it should be bubbly and the
  top brown and crispy.

Hints:

This is good as a main course with a big green salad and a vegetable
  (feeds 4 to 5) or it goes very well as a side dish with a main
  course (serves 6 to 7).

If freezing this dish for another day do it before you bake it.

Notes:

This also can be layered with slices of ham.

My sister Connie pours a large can of stewed tomatoes over
the dish after it comes out of the oven and before she serves it. I
would be shot if I did that to my family but I have served stewed
tomatoes with it and tried spooning them over my serving. It was
delicious.

Heavenly Pot Roast

Just when you thought you had cooked pot roast every way there is, here is one more recipe. This will be a favorite for those who are fond of Beef Stroganoff and for the cook who likes a minimum of work.

What you need:

3-4 lb boneless roast (I use chuck but any will do)
2 tablespoons of olive oil
3/4 cup sour cream
1 teaspoon salt
1 teaspoon pepper
2 cloves garlic smashed and chopped
1 large onion sliced
1 large carrot sliced
3/4 cup dry red wine
3 tablespoons flour
½ cup cold water
juice of ½ lemon

How to assemble:

Sprinkle roast with salt and pepper
In a heavy pot heat the oil and brown the roast on all sides
Remove the roast
Add the onions, garlic and carrot to the hot pot and cook until the
    onions are golden
Add the wine to deglaze pan, stirring all the little browned bits in
    to the broth.

Remove from heat until the broth is not boiling and slowly add the sour cream to the mixture, stirring well

Add meat back to the pot

Cover pot and simmer on very low heat for about 2 ½ hours

Remove meat to a platter and cover with foil to keep warm

Skim off any fat remaining on surface of broth

Mix the flour with the cold water until a smooth paste is formed

Slowly add some of the broth to the paste until is has doubled in quantity

Stir the paste into the pot with the broth

Turn up the heat and stirring constantly bring the mixture to a boil

Cook until thickened to gravy.

Cut the meat into serving size pieces and place in a serving bowl, pour the gravy over the meat or

Serve the gravy separately

You can serve this with rice, potatoes, noodles, or even polenta.

Notes:

Lamb Shanks

If you like lamb you'll love this. It's better than anything you'll find in a restaurant. I researched several cookbooks before finally making up my own recipe. When I make this dish I frequently make a double batch. That's right, for the freezer.

What you need:

4-5 lbs lamb shanks, cracked (approximately 6 shanks)
1 teaspoon salt
1 teaspoon fresh ground pepper
2 teaspoons coarsely ground toasted garlic (or garlic granules)
2 packages of Brown Gravy mix
1 clove of crushed garlic
1 tablespoon of minced parsley
1/8 teaspoon of dried, minced marjoram
dash of ground mace
2 tablespoons of olive oil
2 ½ cups of water

How to assemble:

Rinse shanks and pat dry.
Sprinkle with salt, pepper and garlic granules
Brown shanks well on all sides in the olive oil in a heavy cooking pot or skillet
Add 1 ½ cups of water, cover and simmer for about an hour.
Remove pan from heat

Put lamb shanks on a plate while you finish sauce
Mix 2 envelopes of Brown Gravy mix in 1 cup of cold water
Add gravy to broth in skillet.
Add crushed garlic (or garlic granules), parsley, marjoram and mace.
Put sauce over medium heat and stir until the gravy is thickened.
Add shanks back to gravy.
Cover and cook another hour, until meat is tender.

How to serve:

I love this served with bread stuffing and mint jelly, but Dave prefers it with polenta. Well Dave prefers everything with polenta, but it can also be served with noodles or potatoes.

If you have leftovers, take the meat off the bones and freeze the meat in the gravy for another meal.

Notes:

Lasagna

This is a wonderful meal. Hearty, aromatic, filling and it can be made in advance and only baked prior to serving. The only problem is it feeds a lot of people and even though everyone loves it and eats until almost bursting I have never run out before the eaters got tired of eating. So be prepared to eat it for a couple of meals.

What you need:

Large lasagna baking dish
1 box of lasagna noodles
4 cups of Basic Marinara (see recipe in this book) or the equivalent
    of a commercial sauce
1 pound mushrooms, cleaned and sliced
1 pound of Italian sausage, removed from casings and crumbled
dash of cayenne pepper
1 quart of small curd cottage cheese
2 pounds of Mozzarella cheese, shredded
1 cup grated Parmesean or Asiago cheese
2 cups fresh, dried baby spinach, packed tight (optional)

How to assemble:

Put sauce, sausage and mushroom in a large pot and simmer gently
    until sausage and mushrooms are cooked.
Add a dash of cayenne pepper for a little zing
Set aside to cool

Cook lasagna noodles according to the instructions on the package

Rinse, drain and dry the noodles

Spray the lasagna baking dish liberally with PAM

Assemble all ingredients and begin

Put a thin layer of sauce on the bottom of the pan

Then a layer of noodles, try not to overlap but fill the entire space which might mean you have to cut some noodles to fit

Ladle a layer of sauce with mushrooms and sausage over noodles

Drop spoonfuls of cottage cheese on sauce and spread out, don't worry if it intermingles with sauce

Add a layer of fresh spinach leaves (optional)

Cover the spinach with Mozzarella cheese

Sprinkle with 1/3 grated cheese

Repeat this process with as many layers as will fit in the pan (usually 2 or 3)

The top layer will consist of noodles, sauce and cheese with the rest of the grated cheese on top.

At this point the dish can be frozen, covered and refrigerated until cooking or

Put baking dish in a pre-heated oven at 350° for 1 hour (if cooking a frozen lasagna it may take 1 ½ hours to 2 hours so cover it for the first half of baking time with foil)

Remove from the oven when the top is brown and slightly crusty and let set for ½ hour before serving.

Hints: If you have ingredients leftover use them to make a small lasagna for the freezer.

I sometimes add cooked chicken or turkey pieces to the lasagna

Notes:

Linda's Outstanding Pork Roast

Linda married my brother, Gib, over 40 years ago and is not only my sister-in-law but has been my good friend all those years. Of course I knew she was a good cook, they both cook and I've eaten with them many times. But when Dave and I arrived at their house on our previously mentioned road trip through the South-Western part of the United States, this was in the oven. I don't think we've ever had such a good pork roast. We wondered if it was just the company that made it taste so good but when I got home and did it myself it was still great. How did I live all these years and obviously never really know how to cook pork. This is my new favorite dish for company. Simple, easy and outstanding.

What you need:

8-10 pound shoulder blade pork roast
1 bulb fresh garlic

How to assemble:

Rinse roast and pat dry
Peel 8 or 10 cloves of garlic
Insert knife blade into fleshy part of roast pork and then insert clove of garlic in the slit in the meat, repeat until all garlic is used
Do Not Salt and Pepper the Meat
Lay the roast fat side *down* in a Pyrex or clay roasting dish
Cover tightly with foil
Put the pan in an oven pre-heated to 225°
Cook for 6-8 hours

About 1 ½ hours before serving remove the foil and return the
    roast to the oven to brown
Slice and serve

Notes:

Osso Buco (Veal Shanks)

This is elegant comfort food. I make a pot full and freeze some for another day. In many ways this is similar to cooking lamb shanks but the taste is completely different. Osso Buco is frequently on the menu of the better Italian restaurants and whenever Dave and I find it we usually order it for dinner. But remember that there are many ways to cook this dish and few as good as this recipe so sometimes we're disappointed.

What you need:

4-5 lbs. veal shanks, cracked (approximately 6 shanks)
1 teaspoon salt
1 teaspoon fresh ground pepper
2 teaspoons coarsely ground toasted garlic (or garlic granules)
1 medium brown onion, cubed
1 tablespoon butter
2 tablespoons olive oil
1 cup white table wine
3 packages of Brown Gravy mix
½ cup of fresh or frozen julienned carrots

How to assemble:

Rinse shanks and pat dry.
Sprinkle with salt, pepper and garlic.
In two tablespoons of olive oil brown shanks well on all sides.
When all shanks are browned remove them from the pot
Add a tablespoon of butter to pot and fry a medium to large onion, cubed until caramelized (browned). Deglaze pot with one cup

of white table wine. I use a Chablis. Put the veal shanks back in the pot with the onions and wine and cook on low heat approximately 2 hours.

Add ½ cup of julienned carrots and cook an additional ½ hour. Meat should be falling off the bone.

Remove meat and bones from the pot.

Skim off any fat on top of the broth in the pan

Use 3 envelopes of Brown Gravy mix and stir into 2 cups of cold water.

Stir gravy mix into broth in pan and mix

Cook, stirring constantly, until thickened.

Turn off the heat under pot.

Separate the meat from the bones and skin.

Return the meat to the pot of gravy and discard the rest. (Dave sometimes put the bones in a pot of water and cooks them again for a broth to use in making soup. Or you can freeze them and use them for making soup later.)

Before serving heat up gravy and meat on very low heat. Serve on polenta, mashed potatoes, noodles or rice. Freeze any leftovers for another day. It's great.

Notes:

Paella

The first time I had Paella was a cold, cold day in the Latin Quarter in Paris. That must have been on our first visit in March, 1984. Dave and I had been walking all day and we ducked into this little restaurant to get warm and regroup. They served us Paella for two, crusty tender bread and a pitcher of wine. I thought I was in heaven. It took me a while to find a recipe that was up to my memories and this is it.

I admit that I usually cook this for special occasions or for company. While the contents are a little pricey most of the work can be done before the guests arrive and the final assembly is done only a hour before serving. Additionally, it looks spectacular on the table. I serve it with a very simple salad, see the Caesar Salad recipe in this book, and good bread.

Don't be afraid to vary the ingredients such as adding fish instead of chicken, ham instead of pork and so on. This recipe was originally developed to use up the week's leftovers so any thing goes.

What you need:

1 lb lean boneless pork (cubed)
2 ½ lbs chicken drumettes or 1 lb boneless, skinless chicken breast
    (cubed)
1 ½ lbs. jumbo shrimp, shelled and deveined
2 dozen assorted mussels and clams
½ lb Italian sausage
2-3 tablespoons olive oil
1 large red bell pepper, chopped
2 large onions, chopped
2 cloves of garlic minced

2 cups long grained white rice
1/8 teaspoon of saffron powder or threads
5 cups of chicken broth
1 teaspoon salt
1 cup frozen peas
2 tablespoons finely chopped parsley

How to assemble:

In a large, heavy skillet brown the pork and chicken in the olive oil
then remove from the pan.
Crumble the sausage in the skillet and saute with the onions, garlic
and peppers (If the sausage is in casings remove the casings
before cooking)
Drain the grease from the skillet
*The above steps can be done several hours prior to completion of the
dish. then*
Stir the rice into the sausage mixture and cook until rice looks
opaque.
Stir in the chicken broth, the salt and the saffron
Add the chicken and pork
Bring to boil and let cook uncovered for 20 minutes
Add shrimp, peas and parsley
Cover skillet and reduce fire to low
Cook for 30-40 minutes or until the rice is tender
Uncover and add mussels and clams
Cover and cook for 10 minutes more
Remove dish from heat and let set for 10 minutes so all juices are
absorbed
Put skillet directly on the table and remove lid.

Hints:

I frequently make this in a roasting pan and after the rice boils
for 20 minute I cover the roaster and put it in the oven to finish
cooking. Using that method cook at 350° for 45 minutes before

adding the shellfish. If it is a fancy dinner I will transfer the mixture from the skillet to a large pottery Paella dish before putting it in the oven and cover it tightly with foil.

Notes:

Panuchos

Dave's first wife's family came from the Yucatan Peninsula of Mexico and so many of their dishes are firmly rooted in our family. This is a special dish made from the remains of the Black Bean and Pork dish we're all so fond of. The kids' maternal grandmother apparently turned out dishes like this in a blink of an eye but I confess that it's a major undertaking for us to make it so this is a special occasion dish.

What you need:

2 cups of black beans and pork paste (see recipe in this section)
16 homemade tortillas (see recipe in Cookies, Candies and Baked
   Goods section of this book)
3 to 4 hard boiled eggs, peeled and sliced
1 cup of cooking oil

How to assemble:

In a large skillet cook 3 ½ to 4 cups of black beans and pork down
   until it forms a paste. This should end up with about two
   cups of paste. I suggest you do this after you've served the dish
   and then freeze it until you make the Panuchos.
Follow the recipe in this book for 16 to 20 Tortillas except that
   while you are cooking each tortilla you must tickle it so it will
   puff up.
While the tortilla in on the grill, using the three fingers on one
   hand, gently tickle it in the middle and watch it puff up.
When the tortillas have cooled slightly slit the tortilla at the edge
   so the puffed up section becomes a pocket

Insert about 2 tablespoons of bean paste

Add a slice of boiled egg on top of the paste

Squeeze the slit edge together, use a drop of water to glue it in place

Drop the panuchos in a frying pan of hot oil

When one side is crispy and lightly brown turn over the Panuchos and cook the other side

Drain on paper towels and keep in a warm oven until all are cooked

Serve with salsa and sour cream

Notes:

I have heard that you can add shredded beef, pork or chicken meat on top of the bean paste if you want.

Dave says if you're too lazy to tickle the tortillas you could press them very thin and use two to sandwich the bean paste. I think tickling is fun.

Dave cooks with ease.

Pot Roast

This was the way my mother made pot roast. Imagine my surprise when I found the rest of the world didn't know this recipe. Do it a day ahead or several days ahead, because it takes a while and makes a small mess and there is no sense in causing you to be tired on the day of your dinner.

What you need:

Serves 6-10. Don't worry about leftovers because there is lots to do with them.

large heavy cooking pot
2 or 3 lbs Pork Roast
2 or 3 lbs Chuck Roast
2 tablespoons of olive oil
2 teaspoons salt
2 teaspoons fresh ground pepper
1 teaspoon garlic granules
2 cans of beef broth
5 envelopes of beef or brown gravy mix (Or Cornstarch as appropriate for amount of liquid—see package)

How to assemble:

Sprinkle each side of each roast with salt, pepper and garlic
Brown roasts one at a time in olive oil, starting with the fat side down, making sure all sides are deep brown
When each roast is fully browned remove it from the pan to make room for the next roast

When all roasts are browned set them aside and deglaze the pan used for browning

Pour ½ can of beef broth in the hot pan and stir while bringing the broth to boil, capturing all the browned drippings

Add the roasts and remaining ½ can of beef broth

Simmer 3 or 4 hours until meat is very tender

Note: add more water if necessary but usually the meat will generate sufficient broth

Meat is done when you see it coming off the bones. Cool the meat so you can comfortably remove all fat and bones from roast and cut the meat into chunks, approximately 2" by 2". Store in refrigerator until serving day.

Pour broth in container and refrigerate.

On the serving day remove all congealed fat from broth and discard

Make the gravy in a large pot. I use the appropriate number of envelopes of beef gravy mix, using the broth plus additional canned broth instead of water. Make lots as its very popular. If you prefer your gravy thicker add cornstarch (1 tablespoon) to 1/4 cup cold water and stir it into the gravy mix. When the gravy boils and is the right consistency add the meat and keep on low heat until serving.

Serve with Yorkshire pudding or mashed potatoes, or both.

Hints:

Leftover pot roast can be the beginning of many good things, such as Beef Stroganoff, Beef Pot Pie, and even Chili. Or just freeze it and serve it again as you did the first time.

Notes:

Quiche

This is a family favorite. I always make it for Christmas morning and for Easter. I have evolved the construction of these into a non-working event so as to have them fresh but not take up my time on the Holiday mornings. This recipe is for Quiche Lorraine but I'll include the green chili by putting substitute ingredients in italics. The varieties in this dish are endless by changing the contents and the cheese. You may find another favorite.

Note: These freeze well after baking and can be warmed up either by piece or a whole pie.

What you need:

1 Pillsbury Pie Crust, room temperature and fitted into a Quiche dish or a pie plate
2 cups shredded Jarlsberg cheese (approximate) or *Vermont Cheddar*
1 cup shredded Monterey Jack
1 lb bacon fried crisp and broken into small pieces or *1 small can chopped green chiles, mild*
3 tablespoons flour
3 eggs
½ teaspoon salt
1/16 teaspoon cayenne pepper
1 ½-2 cups milk

How to assemble:

The Day Before:
Prepare Crust

Cook Bacon and Crumble

In a large bowl toss bacon, cheese and flour together or

In a large bowl toss chiles, cheese and flour together

Fill pie or quiche shell with cheese mixture

Cover and refrigerate over night

In the morning:

Pre-heat oven to 400°

In a blender mix eggs, 1 ½ cups of milk, salt and cayenne pepper

Pour egg mixture slowly over cheese mixture giving it time to flow
through the cheese. Liquid needs to be just below the crust
edge to prevent it cooking over in the oven.

If the liquid is too low add milk to bring it to the right point

Put the quiche in the pre-heated oven and bake for 20 minutes at
400°

Turn the oven down to 350° and continue baking for about 30
minutes, the center will be brown and puffed up, when you
insert a knife in the center it will come out clean

Remove from oven and let sit for five minutes before serving.

Hints:

I am usually making 3 or 4 at a time and this method allows me to
do the messy work the day before.

Other variations:

- Shrimp with Jarlsberg
- Caramelized onions with Jarlsberg
- Sauteed spinach and mushrooms with Jarlsberg
- Broccoli and/or cauliflower and cheddar

Notes:

Stuffed Green Peppers

Mitch and Nikki are both good cooks and if you eat at their house who knows who will be cooking what. This recipe of Nikki's is a classic and any of you that love stuffed bell peppers will appreciate knowing how to prepare them.

What you need:

2 lbs ground beef
1 cup uncooked rice
1 egg, beaten
2 tablespoon paprika
1 teaspoon salt or to taste
1 teaspoon pepper or to taste
1 large onion finely chopped
6 to 8 small to medium bell peppers (green)
1 large can tomato juice

How to assemble:

Mix ground beef with rice, egg, salt and pepper, onion and 2
    tablespoons of the paprika and let sit
Wash and dry bell peppers
Carefully core the pepper right around the stem and remove all
    seeds and membrane
Fill each pepper with meat mixture about 2/3's full
Set each filled pepper in deep pot, open side up
Pour tomato juice in pot

Simmer slowly for 2 to 3 hours until meat mixture has expanded
    to fill pepper.
Cool or refrigerate over night
Heat slowly to simmer before serving.

Notes:

Stuffed Zucchini

Of course I've made this. You know I have. I developed this recipe to use up some of the endless zucchini crop. You've heard the zucchini story so you know I probably won't live long enough to want to make it again. But I would eat it if someone else served it because it actually is good. It also freezes but don't keep it more than a few months in the freezer or the zucchini tends to get rubbery.

What you need:

1 ½ lbs ground lamb
1 medium onion, peeled and chopped
1 medium bell pepper, cored, seeded and chopped
3 cloves of garlic, mashed and chopped
2 teaspoons dried sweet basil
1 teaspoon Greek seasoning
1 teaspoon salt
2 cups plain yogurt
1 cup white rice, uncooked
4 8-10 inch zucchini
½ lb Mozzarella cheese, sliced or grated

How to assemble:

Brown the lamb, garlic, onion and bell pepper
Drain off the fat
Add the basil, Greek Seasoning, salt, yogurt and rice
Bring to a boil, then lower the flame and simmer for approximately
    30 minutes until rice is tender and liquid has been absorbed

Slice the zucchini in two, lengthwise

Scoop out the tender flesh in the middle forming an elongated bowl

Chop the zucchini removed from the center and throw it into the mixture of lamb and rice

Fill each zucchini bowl with lamb/rice mixture

Cover each with thin slices of cheese

Set each piece in a baking dish

Pour hot water into the baking dish to cover about ½ inch

Bake in a pre-heated oven at 350°for about 40 minutes until the zucchini is tender and the cheese is brown and bubbly

Remove to serving dish

Notes:

Sweet and Sour Chicken

I had decided to move to San Francisco. I didn't have a job, I didn't know anyone there and I certainly didn't have much money but it was going to be my big adventure. I had my copy of Sex and the Single Girl, *my Dansk candlesticks, my bits and pieces and it was just about time to leave so I decided to give a dinner party. Mom, Dad, Teresa and Nicky went somewhere so I could entertain at the house and I cooked a Chinese dinner. At that time I thought Chinese food was what they served in Chinatown in Los Angeles I've since become much more knowledgeable about Chinese dishes. I made up this recipe and thought I was quite the gourmand. Now I can't even remember who attended that dinner but it must have been successful because I remember it fondly and I served this dish many times after I moved to San Francisco.*

What you need:

1 lb skinless, boneless, cubed chicken
1 medium green bell pepper, seeded and cubed
1 medium onion, cubed
1 medium can pineapple chunks
1 4 oz package of slivered, blanched almonds
1 tablespoon Soy Sauce
1 ½ tablespoon cornstarch
2-3 tablespoon oil
2 tablespoons cider vinegar
2 tablespoons catsup
½ teaspoon dry mustard

Hint:

This recipe works equally well with pork replacing chicken.

How to assemble:

Combine cornstarch and soy sauce in bowl
Stir chicken in mixture and let set for about 15 minutes
Heat oil in wok
Fry chicken a few pieces at a time until chicken is golden brown
Remove chicken to paper to drain
When all chicken is cooked pour off remaining oil leaving only a
    coating in the pan
Using the bowl containing the remaining soy sauce and cornstarch
    mix, pour in the syrup from the can of pineapple
Add the catsup, vinegar and dry mustard and stir to blend—this
    should be a pretty color and have a pungent odor
Heat wok again and stir fry the onion and bell pepper
Stir the bowl containing the sauce and pour into the wok
Cook until the sauce is the right thickness
Taste the sauce and add to adjust ingredients
Add the pineapple chunks and the chicken
Stir over the flame until all the ingredients are hot
Pour into a serving dish and sprinkle almonds over the top
Serve with rice

Notes:

Swiss Steak

My family ate this often and even though I frequently helped make the dish it wasn't my favorite so I never served it to my family. Or maybe it wasn't my favorite because I did help make it, pounding the flour into the steak is hard work but necessary to tenderize it and ensure the flavor. But this was my cousin, Barb's, favorites so Mom would make it when she was coming to dinner. And it's a good example of tasty old fashion cooking, it turns a cheap cut of meat into a delicious meal.

What you need:

3-4 lbs of chuck or round steak
½ cup flour (more if needed)
salt
pepper
3 medium onions, sliced
1 14oz can stewed chopped tomatoes

How to assemble:

Lay the steak on a cutting board and remove excess fat and any
    bones (keep the fat to render down to brown the meat)
Sprinkle the meat generously with flour, salt and pepper
Using a small saucer edge pound the flour into the steak
Add more flour and turn steak, pounding from another direction
Turn the steak over and repeat this process
Do each side one more time—The steak should look thinner and
    very rough and most of the flour is pounded into the meat

Take the trimmed fat and put it into a large hot skillet, rendering it down so a layer of fat covers the skillet bottom

Cut the pounded meat into serving size pieces, approximately 4" x 5"

Brown each side of each piece of meat in the hot skillet

Remove browned meat to make room to brown the next pieces

Add olive oil if necessary to continue browning the meat

When all the meat is browned and removed from the skillet lay the onion slices in the remaining fat and brown them

When the onions are becoming translucent put the meat back into the skillet on top of the onions

Pour the can of stewed tomatoes over the meat

Cover the skillet

Lower the heat and simmer for 1 ½ to 2 hours or until meat is very tender

Serve with mashed potatoes

Hint:

You can have your chuck steak boned and tenderized at the market and then you only have dip it in flour on each side before browning. But it won't taste quite the same. However, considering the work and the mess, taste may be a small sacrifice.

Notes:

Tamale Pie

When I was little, maybe nine, my mother took all five of us kids on the old Red Car to Los Angeles to see where my Dad worked and to have dinner. This was a big deal. We never went out to dinner. It was too expensive and people just didn't do it, at least the people we knew. Anyway, we went to Clifton's Cafeteria on Olive and 5th in Los Angeles. Decorated with waterfalls, palm trees and neon lights, it was like a nightclub, they even had a photographer who went around taking pictures. Our picture is on the front of this book. To a little kid, Clifton's had endless counters of food to select. I didn't know what to choose, afraid to take something in case something better was further down the line but I worried I would get to the end with nothing. And that panicked me. Finally, I picked what Connie picked, Tamale Pie. It was the first time I had it and it was wonderful, or maybe the whole experience was wonderful. Anyway, Tamale Pie has great memories for me and besides it's a simple, nutritious meal.

What you need:

1 ½ lbs of lean ground beef
1 medium onion, chopped
1 clove of garlic, minced
2 tablespoon chili powder
1 tablespoon cumin
1 teaspoon salt
1 16 oz can stewed tomatoes
1 8 oz can tomato sauce
1 can pitted black olives, drained
1 cup yellow corn meal

1/3 cup oil
1 egg, beaten
1 17 oz can cream style yellow corn
1 teaspoon baking powder

How to assemble:

Brown meat, onion, garlic and salt
Drain off fat
Add stewed tomatoes, tomato sauce and spices
Simmer about 20 minutes
Stir in olives and pour into a 2 quart, greased baking dish
Mix cornmeal, baking powder, corn, oil and egg
Pour over top of meat mixture
Bake in 350° oven for 45 minutes or until crust is done.

Variations:

Try using leftover pot roast, pork roast, chicken or turkey in this
    dish, use 3 cups diced or shredded cooked meat in place of the
    ground meat
Add meat after browning the onions and garlic

Notes:

Teriyaki Chicken or Steak

Years ago, in the late '60's my hippy friend insisted I join her and a couple of her artist friends at a party in the East Bay. I don't know why I let her talk me into it because I was always very careful of getting trapped somewhere strange with no way to get home. But I went. And surprisingly this was a very traditional house warming with pretty normal people. The host had marinated thin slices of beef in this sauce for two days before cooking them on the barbeque and the meat was the best I've ever had. So it turns out that I had a nice day, met some new people and ended up with this recipe which I've used ever since.

I use it to marinade London Broil before grilling it. I use it for marinading chicken, which is a big family favorite, before cooking it on the barbeque. And I save it between uses as it only gets better. Store leftover marinade in the freezer, clearly marked as to whether it has been used for chicken or beef.

Caution: Do not use chicken marinade on beef next time around at its liable to carry germs to the beef which frequently isn't as well cooked as the chicken. Also, if using the marinade with chicken never taste it. Even if the chicken has been rinsed it might have bacteria that can cause illness similar to food poisoning. Cooking the meat kills that potentially dangerous bacteria.

What you need:

1 cup soy sauce
3 cups white wine (Chablis or other table wine)
1/4 cup of fresh ginger sliced and/or chopped
1 whole garlic with cloves smashed and peeled
2 tablespoons sugar

How to assemble:

In a large bowl or pot mix the above ingredients and then add the
meat to marinade.

Cover the dish and refrigerate

Cover the dish and refrigerate (I defrost chicken parts in the marinade)

Try to cover the meat completely but if not possible turn the meat
a couple of times during the marinade process

Marinade the meat at least overnight and preferably for a whole
day prior to barbequing

After placing the meat on the grill pour the marinade, including
the garlic and ginger into a container. Remove any bits of meat
left in the broth.

Label clearly and place in the freezer until next time.

You can use this marinade 2 to 3 times before discarding.

Notes:

Grill meat the way you would normally, consult your grill's
cookbook for details.

Thanksgiving Turkey

As a child, Thanksgiving was my favorite day. We always had it at our house and it wasn't until I was much older that I wondered how my parents managed it. Where did they get the plates and silverware? How, when our finances had so many ups and downs, did they afford to put on this dinner year after year? All the relatives came and during the fifties and sixties there would always be 20 to 30 people there. But it was a great day and filled with enough memories to last through my life.

When Dave and I met it was just one more coincidence that we each cooked Thanksgiving dinner every year and we each cooked the turkey on the barbeque. If you haven't done this you should try it. Not only is the turkey delicious but it keeps the kitchen free for cooking the supporting dishes. Over the years we have refined the process, cooking the turkey on the barbeque and the stuffing in the oven. This recipe explains our method but you can always put your turkey on a rack, in a roasting pan with about a cup of water in the bottom. Bake it in an oven at 500° for ½ hour, then reduce the temperature to 325° and continue to cook until the turkey is done. Use a meat thermometer or shake a leg to see if it's loose.

Or try this.

What you need:

1 turkey (28-31 lb turkey)
1 medium onion, peeled and quartered
1 large apple, quartered

Gravy:
turkey innards
2 stalks of celery with leaves
1 medium onion, peeled and quartered
6 cans chicken broth
2 tablespoons olive oil
8 packages turkey gravy mix
1-2 tablespoons cornstarch

How to assemble:

Set up barbeque with the indirect heating method (coals on either
    side, drip pan in the middle. (If you want a hickory smoked
    flavor add hickory chips, soaked in water to the coals periodically)
Remove the innards from the turkey and set aside
Pull any pin feathers and discard
Dry the turkey inside and out
Set the turkey breast side down in a rack, sprayed with PAM
Put the quartered apple and onion in the cavity
Cover the wings and leg tips with aluminum foil
Set rack with turkey over a throw away drip pan, cover barbeque
    and cook
Check every few hours and add hot coals as necessary (we start
    coals in another pan so that when we add, we're adding hot
    coals)
A thirty lb turkey takes 4-5 hours
One hour from finish, remove the foil from the wings and leg tips
When the turkey is done, let it sit on platter, covered with foil for
    about ½ hour before carving.

Gravy:
In a large, heavy pot brown the innards in the hot oil
Deglaze pot with chicken broth, making sure to capture all the
    brown bits in the pot

Add the celery and onion to the pot

Add a total of 2 cans of chicken broth

Simmer for 2-3 hours

When gizzard, heart and liver are tender strain the pot reserving both the liquid and the innards, discard the celery and onion

If your family likes giblet gravy, cut up the innards to be added to the gravy

If your family likes the giblets as appetizers, cut them up, salt and pepper them and pass them around.

Defat the broth and return the broth to the pot

Add all the chicken broth but reserve one can

Use the last can to dissolve the gravy mixes into a smooth paste, then slowly add to the pot mixing well

Bring the gravy to a boil, stirring constantly

Reduce to a simmer and stir until it reaches your favorite consistency.

If necessary to thicken, dissolve 1 tablespoon cornstarch in 3 tablespoons cold water to smooth paste

Add a little hot gravy continuing to stir, than add cornstarch mix to gravy

Let simmer until thickened, if still not thick enough repeat this step

Notes:

Mitch's bird, it's a hereditary thing.

Turkey Mole

When you are "Turkeyed" out but you still have more in the freezer you might want to try this recipe. It's not like any turkey recipe you've used and it's good in tacos, burritos or even served with rice as a main dish.

What you need:

1/4 cup of butter or oleo
1 small onion, minced
2 garlic cloves smashed and minced
1/4 cup tomato paste
½ cup slivered almonds, minced
1/4 cup chili powder
1 tablespoon oregano
1 tablespoon unsweetened cocoa powder
½ teaspoon cinnamon
½ teaspoon ground cloves
½ teaspoon ground nutmeg
½ teaspoon ground allspice
½ teaspoon groung ginger
½ teaspoon ground cumin
1 cup turkey stock or canned chicken broth
4 cups of coarsely shredded turkey meat

How to assemble:

In a large sauce pan melt the butter and saute onions and garlic
    until they are soft
Add the tomato paste, turkey broth and all the seasonings and mix well

Bring mixture to a boil
Reduce heat and simmer for about five minutes
Add turkey meat and cook until turkey is hot
Serve

Notes:

Turkey Tortilla Casserole

This is a great use of leftover turkey but you could also use chicken. The first time I made this I inadvertently used hot chiles instead of mild ones. It says a lot about this dish that it was still pretty popular at those famous Sunday dinners in spite of gasps and tears caused by my choice of chillies the first time I served it. By the way, this is another of the recipes I got from my friend Margaret.

What you need:

1 dozen corn tortillas
2 tablespoons of dried onion flakes
½ cup milk
1 can cream of mushroom soup
1 can cream of chicken soup
1 cup sour cream
1 small can of chopped green chiles (mild)
4 cups of cooked, cubed turkey (or chicken)
½ teaspoon dried garlic granules
1 small can of sliced black olives, drained
½ lb of Monterey Jack cheese, grated (1 ½ cups)

How to assemble:

Tear the tortillas into small pieces (the approximate size of the
    turkey cubes)
Combine in a large bowl the tortillas with all of the other
    ingredients in the order listed

Spread the mixture in a greased, large baking pan
Sprinkle the cheese evenly over the top
Bake uncovered in a pre-heated 350° oven for 40 to 45 minutes
Serves about 6

Notes:

Vanya's Cabbage Rolls

Vanya's mother used to make cabbage rolls during the holidays. They smelled vile but tasted heavenly. This was a traditional dish from Croatia and if you've ever had it you understand how great it was.

Later on one of my visits with Vanya in San Diego she cooked this version. By then she was already an accomplished chef and she had worked on her mother's recipe to reduce the fat and to simplify the preparation. Using her recipe, even I could produce this dish on occasion and I did on lots of occasions until Mitch met and married Nikki, also a Croatian. After that Nikki supplied our family with the real thing at all the holidays. (See Nikki's recipe following this.)

What you need:

2 lb ground turkey
2 lbs Italian sausage
1 cup uncooked rice
2 eggs, beaten
4-5 cloves of garlic, smashed and chopped
1 tablespoon Spice Islands Fine Herbs
1 teaspoon salt
1 teaspoon pepper
2 large onions
1 large head cabbage
1 large jar sauerkraut
4 cups chicken stock

How to assemble:

Brown all the Italian sausages except four, cut each browned sausage
   into four pieces and set aside
Remove the casings from the 4 sausages not browned
Mix that sausage meat with the ground turkey
Add the rice, eggs, garlic, herbs, salt and pepper
Mix thoroughly and let sit
Carefully remove the outer cabbage leaves and rinse them.
Cook the cabbage leaves a few at a time in the microwave until the
   leaves are soft and malleable but not completely limp
Let the leaves cool while you are preparing more
Spoon about 1/3 cup of meat mixture into each cabbage leaf
Roll each leaf around the meat mixture loosely to leave room for the
   filling to expand when the rice cooks. Tuck the sides inside and
   set the roll on its seam. (If the core of the leaves are a problem in
   forming a nice roll, simply cut it out before forming the roll.)
Continue with this process until all the meat has been used
Shred all the remaining cabbage and place in a large container
Peel and slice the onions and add to the cabbage
Drain the sauerkraut and add to the cabbage
Mix the cabbage, onion and sauerkraut well
In a large cooking pot lay a layer of the cabbage mixture on the bottom
Put a layer of cabbage rolls on the cabbage,
Place pieces of the browned sausage amongst the cabbage rolls
Add another layer of cabbage, cabbage rolls and sausage until all
   have been used, the last layer should be cabbage.
Pour the chicken broth over the layers.
Simmer gently about 2 hours
Cool overnight
Before serving, heat slowly and simmer 1 ½ hours.
NEVER STIR THE POT as you'll break up the cabbage rolls

Goes very well with mashed potatoes.

Notes:

Yugoslavian Cabbage Rolls

This is a traditional Croatian dish. Mitch's wife, Nikki, makes them for us every holiday season. You don't have to be Croatian to enjoy them. This recipe produces a dish that is an act of love. Nikki invites you to create her masterpiece but don't plan to eat them the day you cook them. It takes about three days for the flavor to set and for them to be perfect.

What you need:

2 lb ground beef
1 cup uncooked rice
1 eggs, beaten
4-5 cloves of garlic, smashed and chopped
4 tablespoon paprika
1 teaspoon salt or to taste
1 teaspoon pepper or to taste
1 large onion finely chopped
2 large head cabbage
1 large jar sauerkraut 32oz.
vinegar

How to assemble:

Mix ground beef with rice, egg, garlic, salt and pepper, onion and
    2 tablespoons of the paprika and let sit
Boil the cabbage, one head at a time in a mixture of 1 part vinegar
    to 4 parts of water. Vinegar/water should cover head.
When the outer cabbage leaves become opaque and flexible carefully
    cut them loose and remove them from the pot to cool

When all the large leaves have been cooked removed and discard
the rest of the cabbage head and prepare the second head in
the same manner.

Forming the Cabbage Rolls:
Select a cabbage leaf and cut the thick core out
Spoon about 1/3 cup of meat mixture into each cabbage leaf
Fold the bottom of the leaf over the meat then roll the leaf loosely
around the mixture to allow for the meat and rice to expand in
cooking
Tuck the top of the leaf down into the roll
Continue with this process until all the meat has been used

Cooking instructions:
In a large cooking pot place ½ of the cabbage rolls in a layer on the
bottom
Put ½ the jar of sauerkraut on top of the cabbage rolls
Add the rest of the cabbage rolls and then another layer of
sauerkraut
Add the juice from the sauerkraut and enough water to reach the
top of the cabbage rolls
Sprinkle the remaining two tablespoons of paprika over the top
Simmer for 3 hours
Refrigerate over night
Next day simmer 2 hours and refrigerate again
When serving bring to a slow simmer and then serve.

*Cabbage rolls should not be served until the third day as the flavors
need that time to meld and develop.*

Notes:

When heating or cooking NEVER STIR this dish as it only
breaks the cabbage rolls apart. Just heat slowly and then enjoy.

A family birthday dinner with Mitch, his wife,
Nikki, and Miles.

The Pud
(Desserts)

*At a Coates family gathering in Michigan. Here is our
cousin, Gayle(little Gayle), Gayle (me), Connie and
Teresa.*

CONTENTS

Aunt Nell's Special Torte Cake

Aunt Nell was my mother's oldest sister. She and her husband, Lee, used to come out from Chicago for grand visits until finally they drove their big Hudson out in 1953, settling in Monrovia. Then they were close enough to join us for all our holidays and they always went out of their way to contribute generously to the occasion. Every Christmas she arrived loaded with presents and goodies, including home made popcorn balls and this cake. Food processors were non-existent in those days so this layered torte cake was an act of love. It still is so special it should be reserved for those occasions where it can be thoroughly appreciated, not just a taste of sweet tacked on to a great meal.

What you need:

2 round Pyrex cake pans, a mixer and a Cuisanart or other food
   processor with a disk for fine grating

Cake:
1 cup of grated unsweetened German Chocolate
1/2 pound of sweet butter (unsalted) room temperature
1 cup cake flour (this is usually finer than the regular)
1 teaspoon of baking powder
6 eggs at room temperature, separated
2 tablespoons of water
1 cup of sugar
½ teaspoon salt
1 teaspoon vanilla

Icing:

1 cup of boiled milk poured over

1 cup of finely grated walnuts then cooled to room temperature

1 cup of sweet butter

2 cups of powdered sugar

How to assemble:

Set oven at 350°

Get pans ready by spraying with PAM, lining the pans with wax paper and spraying again

Making the Cake:

Beat yolks, adding 2 tablespoons of water and ½ cup of sugar until they are thick and lemon colored. Set aside.

Beat egg whites, when foaming, slowly add salt, vanilla and ½ cup of sugar.

Beat until whites hold soft peaks.

Fold yolk mixture into whites then

Fold flour and baking powder in

Fold in grated chocolate.

Spread mixture evenly in the two pans and bake for 20 minutes.

Let cool ten minutes then turn out on a rack, pull paper from bottom and continue to let cool.

When cool take a long serrated bread knife and cut through each cake layer so you now have four layers.

Making the Icing:

Do this while your cake is cooling.

Cream the butter

Add the powdered sugar slowly and beat until mixture is almost white.

Add nut/milk mixture slowly and continue beating until the mixture is now the consistency of whipped cream.

Use 1/4 of icing to cover top and sides of first layer, repeat three more times. Be sure to always put the cut side of the cake down so when you spread the icing you won't make crumbs.

When the cake is iced, smooth your knife along the sides, add any decorations you wish, halves of walnuts, a rose bud dipped in foaming egg white and then sugar or anything you like. Keep refrigerated until serving.

This cake can be frozen. So make ahead of time or keep the leftovers for another special occasion

Notes:

Aunt Nell, Emma's oldest child and my favorite Aunt.

Caramel Apple Bread Pudding

This is to die for. One year Dave and I went on the Chefs Tour sponsored by Macy's and we selected the Boulevard with Nancy Oakes as Chef. We had the most marvelous lunch and for desert she made bread pudding. I am always a sucker for bread pudding but never can get it right when I make it. It's funny that I feel my bread pudding never tastes as good as my mother made, and my mother always complained that her's didn't match her mother's. But after watching Nancy and making some adjustments I think this one is a winner. By the way, my mother finally concluded that her's wasn't as good as her mother's because her mother used leftover home made bread. Nancy used brioche but I usually use a good french bread. Take the time to find the right bread.

What you need:

1 quart baking dish
4 Pippin or Gravenstein apples, peeled and sliced
8 slices of sweet french bread, ½ inch thick
2 cups brown sugar, tightly packed
1 cup butter
10 egg yolks, beaten well
4 cups heavy cream
1 cup granulated sugar
2 teaspoons real vanilla
1 teaspoon cinnamon
1/4 teaspoon cloves
1/4 teaspoon nutmeg
½ cup raisins (optional)

How to assemble:

In a sauce pan gently simmer the cream
In a bowl mix the egg yolks with the sugar and beat
Remove the cream from the fire
Slowly mix the egg yolk into the simmering cream
Add the vanilla, stir and set aside
Melt the butter and brown sugar in a large skillet over medium heat
Add the apple slices and simmer until apples are soft but still hold
    their shape
Sprinkle the apples with cinnamon, cloves and nutmeg
Spray baking dish with PAM
Cut the crusts off the bread
Cover the bottom of the baking dish with bread
Spoon custard over each slice
Lay slices of apple on each slice of bread and drizzle caramel sauce
    over the first layer
If you are using raisins, scatter them over the apples
Lay a second slice of bread over the apples
Spoon the rest of the custard evenly over the bread using up all the
    custard
Place the baking dish in a larger shallow pan and place in the oven
Pour hot water in the larger pan so that it comes halfway up the
    side of the custard dish
Bake in a preheated oven at 250° until pudding is golden brown
    and a knife inserted in the pudding comes out clean

Serve warm with whipped cream or ice cream

Notes:

Chocolate Crazy Cake

I think my mother liked to make this because it 's just a crazy way to make a cake. We liked it because it was just plain good.

What you need:

1 ½ cups flour
1 cup sugar
3 tablespoons unsweetened cocoa powder
½ teaspoon salt
1 teaspoon baking soda
6 tablespoons vegetable oil
1 teaspoon vanilla
1 tablespoon white or cider vinegar
1 cup water

How to assemble:

Use a 9" square cake pan, ungreased
Mix the flour, sugar, cocoa, salt and soda in the pan
Make three dents in the dry mixture with a spoon
In each dent pour one of the following: vinegar, oil and vanilla
Pour the water over the top
Using a fork mix it all together
Put the pan in a pre-heated oven at 350° for about 30 minutes
Cool and serve

This cake can be frosted or just sprinkle powdered sugar on top

Notes:

Chocolate Pudding

Did you know that you can actually make pudding? It doesn't have to come out of a can or a box. When we were kids we made pudding frequently because the main ingredient was milk and we always had lots of that on hand. But if you want more credit for your efforts you can truthfully call this a mousse and then people will be more impressed. Layer the pudding with whipped cream or put it in a fancy glass instead of using a bowl and see how good it looks and tastes. I guarantee it will taste great.

What you need:

2 cups of milk
2 eggs separated
½ cup of sugar
4 tablespoons flour
1/4 teaspoon salt
2 tablespoons unsweetened cocoa powder
1 teaspoon vanilla

How to assemble:

In a large heavy pan heat milk to just about boiling
In a bowl combine egg yokes, sugar, flour, cocoa, salt
Add a small amount of hot milk and make a paste
Add paste slowly to pan of milk
Bring to a boil stirring constantly and boil 5 minutes
Remove from heat and cool
Meanwhile whip egg whites to form stiff peaks
Fold egg whites into still warm pudding

Pour pudding into glasses or bowls
Cool and serve—makes four servings

Notes:

Dave Limp's Fantastic Pie Crust

I had heard Danielle's husband Dave mention that he baked pies but didn't really pay much attention until he brought an apple pie and a chocolate pie to our last Thanksgiving dinner. They looked like a cover shoot for Bon Appetite and tasted even better than they looked. It was the crust. It was fantastic and its because of a secret ingredient. If you like pie or know someone who does you have to try this. And by the way, you can always invite me, I love pie.

What you need:

2 cups flour
1 teaspoon salt
3/4 cup Crisco
3 tablespoons cold orange juice
2 tablespoons cold water
9" pie pan

How to assemble:

Mix flour and salt
Cut Crisco into flour with two knives until pebbly (size of small peas)
Sprinkle with water/orange juice
Gather and work dough together until it forms a ball
Chill the dough for 45 minutes
Divide in two balls, one slightly larger than the second
Roll out the larger ball of dough between two pieces of wax paper, turning after each roll until dough forms a circle approximately 12" in diameter.

Peel off one piece of wax paper and lay the crust in a pie plate, gently pushing it down to fit the plate

Peel off the second layer of wax paper

Roll out the second half of dough the same way but setting it aside in the wax paper until the filling has been added to the pie

Add your selected filling to the prepared pie plate (you might want to use the Strawberry-Rhubarb recipe from this section of the book)

Remove one sheet of wax paper from the remaining pie crust and lay the exposed crust over the filled pie plate.

Remove the second sheet of was paper

Move around the pie plate crimping the edges together then trimming off the leftover edge

Fork the crust for ventilation and sprinkle lightly with sugar

Bake in a 350° pre-heated oven until crust is brown and filling has thicken and is bubbling, cooking time will depend on filling.

Notes:

Foolproof Pie Crust

I use the Pillsbury pie crust already formed and folded into quarters but should you want the credit for producing the crust yourself then try this. Actually, it probably tastes better than Pillsbury but as I don't usually eat the pie crust, just the innards, I don't notice. Granny (that's what all the grandchildren called my mother) was famous for her pies. But I never remember a pie she didn't say disparagingly as she was serving it, "Well, I don't know how the crust will come out." It always came out tender and flakey. Never-the-less, she switched to this recipe in the late 70's and it must have been good as she used this ever after.

What you need:

3 cups flour
1 teaspoon salt
1 teaspoon sugar
1 ½ cups Crisco
1 egg
1 tablespoon white vinegar
5 tablespoons water

How to assemble:

Mix together the flour, salt and sugar
Using a fork, two table knives or a pastry blender cut in the Crisco
In a small bowl beat the egg, vinegar and water together
Add liquid in small amounts to flour mixture mixing it with your fork
until the dough pulls away from the bowl into a ball (Note: you
may have to add more flour or water to reach the right consistency)

Divide dough into two balls

Turn one ball of dough out on a floured board and roll into a 10" round.

Place in pie plate, turn the excess edge under and use your thumb to make a decorative border around the rim. (If the excess is too much to turn under, trim it off. Dave likes this crust baked with a little sugar sprinkled on top. Or children like to cut it into shapes before baking it.)

Repeat the process for the top crust, or the second pie bottom. Don't forget that if you're using a top crust you must cut air holes to let the steam escape.

Bake in a 350° until crust is brown and filling has thicken and is bubbling, cooking time will depend on filling.

Hints:

Two crust pies are usually used for fruit pies such as apple, berry or cherry, and meat pies such as turkey or beef pot pies. One crust pies are used for quiches, custard, cream pies and etc.

Crusts to be used for pies with pudding filling such as Lemon, banana cream, chocolate are baked empty and filled later. Don't forget to prick the crust bottom with a fork to vent for steam to escape during cooking or the crust will puff up out of shape.

Notes:

Fruit Cake

I know, I know all the stories about fruit cakes but I actually like fruit cake. And Dave use to make fruit cakes to give away every Christmas and he still gets a hurt look when someone jokes about fruit cakes. But this is not the traditional fruit cake in dark batter, soaked for months in rum or other equally potent brew. This is a light, fruity concoction that is more like desert than a cake.

What you need:

1 lb stoned dates, chopped (pitted)
1 lb pecan or walnut pieces
½ cup candied cherries, chopped
½ cup candied pineapple, chopped
4 eggs
1 cup sugar
1 cup flour
2 teaspoons baking powder
1 teaspoon vanilla

How to assemble:

Beat eggs until they are light and frothy
Add sugar, flour and vanilla and continue beating
Fold in the fruit and nuts
Sprinkle the baking powder over the batter and stir it in
Spray an angel food pan with PAM and pour in the batter
Bake in a pre-heated oven at 300° for 1 hour and 15 minutes

Remove and let cool slightly
Invert pan over a cake plate and cool completely
Serve warm with whipped cream

Notes:

Lace Baskets

When Danielle was fourteen we decided to take her with us on our annual trip to England. Of course we visited Dave's favorite cousins, Liz and Quent and their two girls. Liz is a wonderful cook and did herself proud with the dinner. Danielle asked for seconds of the steak and kidney pie and never even asked what a kidney was. Anyway, when it came to the pud, Liz and her daughter, Emma, served this lace basket with an orange pudding in it. Danielle somehow conned Liz out of her recipe book and so we had to learn to make these baskets, too. They're a little tricky to form so expect to ruin the first few but it doesn't take long to get the knack and then you have a desert that will knock the socks off your guests.

Several years later on a subsequent visit we were talking about that desert and Liz admitted that she had given the book to Danielle thinking she could easily replace it as it was a Sainsbury book but she had never found it again. So when I got home I copied the recipes for Danielle and returned the original to Liz so she could again make those great deserts.

What you need:

4 tablespoons butter or margarine
4 tablespoons of coarse brown sugar
4 tablespoons of golden syrup (Karo Light Brown)
4 tablespoons of flour

How to assemble:

Heat butter, sugar and syrup in a pan until butter is melted and
  sugar is dissolved

Cool slightly

Beat in flour (If you like crunchy add a handful of nuts here)

Divide dough into twelve scoops

Place only four on one cookie sheet

Bake at 350° degrees for about 12 minutes, until golden

Remove from oven and cool slightly

Remove from pan with pallette knife and gently press over the inverted end of a glass, forming a basket

Let cool then gently remove

Just before serving fill with ice cream or pudding

Notes:

I sometimes spray the glass with PAM to assist in removing the Lace Basket. I find that the first couple baskets don't look so good but then I get the hang of it. Don't try to cook more than four at a time or they get too cool before you get them formed into baskets.

Liz and Quent, some of Dave's English cousins.

Lemon Blueberry Pound Cake

This tastes as good as it sounds. I made this cake when our friend, Al Ujcic, was visiting and as if it wasn't good enough by itself, I topped it with mixed berries and whipped cream. It didn't take long for us to polish off the entire cake. I'm sure it would freeze well but so far I've never had the chance to see.

What you need:

1 cup of butter, room temperature
1 cup of granulated sugar
4 large eggs separated
1 tablespoon finely grated lemon zest (yellow peel of lemon)
1 teaspoon vanilla
3/4 cup sour cream
1 ½ cups all-purpose flour
pinch of salt
2 cups fresh or defrosted blueberries, patted dry

How to assemble:

Preheat oven to 350°
Spray a loaf pan or a small fluted copper mold with PAM
Cream butter and sugar together until light and fluffy
Add egg yolks, lemon zest and vanilla and beat until smooth
Beat in the sour cream until mixed thoroughly
Mix together the flour, baking powder and salt
Using three batches mix the flour mixture into the previous bowl
    until just combined
In a separate bowl beat the egg whites until they hold soft peaks

Stir a third of the whites into the batter until combined, then fold in the remaining whites being careful not to over mix.

Fold in the blueberries

Pour into pan and bake for 35 minutes

Turn down the temperature of the oven to 325° and bake for 45 minutes longer or until a toothpick inserted in the middle comes out clean

Cool on a rack for about an hour before turning out of the pan.

Notes:

Miniature Cheesecakes

This is a perfect recipe for an afternoon tea or to take to a potluck. Or just make it for the holiday buffet. One of Danielle's high school friends gave me this recipe when I was preparing for our annual tree decorating party. It worked so well I've made them many times since. Not only are they easy, tasty, and look great. It's a finger food.

What you need:

24 cup cake cup liners
24 Vanilla Wafer cookies
16 oz softened cream cheese
3/4 cup sugar
2 eggs
1 tablespoon fresh lemon juice
1 teaspoon vanilla
1 can cherry or blueberry pie filling

How to assemble:

Place a liner in each hole of the appropriate number of muffin tins
Put a vanilla wafer cookie in the bottom of each with the flat side down
Beat the cream cheese, eggs, sugar, lemon juice and vanilla until
    smooth and creamy
Pour mixture over the cookie until the cupcake liner is 2/3 full
Bake in a pre-heated oven at 375° for 15-20 minutes, until cheese
    filling is set
Remove and cool
Spoon your choice of pie filling on each cheesecake or use the Nut

Crunch Topping. You may want to use a variety.
Chill for at least three hours before serving.

Notes:

Mocha Bombe

In our family every birthday is celebrated at a Sunday dinner and the Birthday person selects the menu. That sometimes got pretty tricky for Dave and I but we somehow managed to always deliver what was requested. The year after we took Danielle with us to England she presented us with one of our greater challenges. We knew we were in trouble when she got the cookbooks out to help her select her menu. Finally she selected Chicken Cordon Bleu, Dave's rice pilaf, Gayle's signature salad and this desert from Liz's English cook book. And of course, since it was summer we had a houseful of guests as well as the extended family to serve. But I have to admit that this was one of our more memorable meals.

While we didn't make the Cordon Bleu often after that we did serve the Mocha Bombe several times. It looks elegant and tastes wonderful. You'll have a hard time convincing people that you made it. It's amazingly easy. Remember the Bon-Bons you use to buy in the movies? Now think bigger. That's the idea.

What you need:

8 oz milk chocolate or semi-sweet chocolate
2 tablespoons of instant coffee granules
2 tablespoons of boiling water
2 egg whites
½ cup white sugar
1 cup whipping cream

How to assemble:

Select a nicely shaped bowl that holds more than a quart and place
    it in the freezer to chill
Break up the chocolate in the upper pan of a double boiler and
    melt it over the hot water
Remove the bowl from the freezer and pour the melted chocolate
    into the bowl, rotating it so that all the sides have an even
    layer of chocolate
Return the bowl to the freezer until the filling is ready
Mix the coffee granules with the boiling water then let cool
Beat the egg whiles until they're stiff, gradually whisk in the sugar
    and then set aside
Pour the cooled coffee in the whipping cream and then whip to soft peaks
Fold the egg whites into the coffee cream
Spoon the mixture into the bowl lined with chocolate, smoothing
    the top evenly.
Cover the bowl and return to the freezer
Freeze until firm, approximately 3 hours
Dip the basin (bowl) into cool water briefly and invert on serving
    plate, you may have to give it a sharp shake to loosen the bombe
Cut it in wedges, keep hot water in a glass to insert your knife so
    you can cut cleanly

Notes:

Don't like mocha? Use instant chocolate mix.

Or feeling lazy? Use your favorite ice cream to fill the chocolate
shell. Let the ice cream soften a bit before filling the shell and then
harden again in the freezer before serving.

And don't forget if you have plenty of freezer space you could
keep a couple of chocolate coated bowls there for last minute
surprises.

One time I used little custard cups to make individual bombe's
that way I didn't have to cut them.

Mom's Raisin Cake

Try this on a dank, cold day and create the same memories we had as children, arriving home to wonderful smells and anticipation of this spicy delicious treat. When Mom baked this we didn't have to wait until dinner to try it, she always cut us a chunk warm from the oven. Maybe she didn't want to wait either. One day Mom made the mistake of mixing up a little icing for it and my Dad always asked for it iced from then on, but I prefer it just plain, warm and with a big glass of cold milk.

When I went through Emma's note book I found this recipe, so now we know where it came from, but to me it's Mom's cake so that is why it is in this part of the book.

What you need:

9 x 13 baking pan, sprayed with PAM.
2 quart sauce pan 1 lb of raisins (you can add dried cherries, cranberries or any other dried fruit you wish)
2 cups sugar
½ cup of butter or margarine
1 teaspoon cinnamon
1 teaspoon cloves
1/4 teaspoon nutmeg
1 teaspoon salt
2 cups of hot water
1 teaspoon baking soda
1 cup cold water
3 ½ cups of flour
2 teaspoons baking powder
1 cup of nut meats

How to assemble: (this cake is made in 4 steps)

Set oven for 350°

1. Place fruit, sugar, spices, butter and salt in water in the sauce
    pan and bring to a boil
        Boil for 10 minutes and remove from the heat
2. Dissolve the baking soda in the cold water and add to boiled
    mixture, stirring well. This will cause the mixture to bubble
    and foam.
3. Combine the flour and baking powder
        Add small amounts of boiled mixture to the flour stirring
    well to remove lumps until the batter is completely mixed.
4. Add nuts, optional

Pour into the baking pan and bake until done (approximately 45
    minutes). Insert a toothpick in the center of the cake, if the
    toothpick does not have any batter sticking to it when it is
    removed the cake is done.
Cool.

How to serve:

Warm or cold, iced or plain, it is a winner and the house will
smell good for hours.
    The entire cake is a total of 4600 calories without frosting. So
if you cut the cake 6 x 4 it will be 190 calories a piece.

Notes:

Pineapple Upside Down Cake

I think I've made this cake forever. I know that I made it when I was in the fifth or sixth grade because the first time I used a cake mix was to make this cake. I was so stupid that when the box said add the remaining milk, I put the rest of the bottle of milk in it. Somehow that seemed to make sense to me. My mother didn't even get mad even though I had committed the unpardonable sin, I wasted good food.

Anyway whether you use a boxed cake or one from scratch this is a winner every time you serve it. Mom had a big old cast iron black skillet that I used for this cake. But since I no longer have one I make do with a frying pan for the carmelization and then transfer it to a baking dish before laying out the fruit and adding the cake batter.

What you need:

1/4 cup of butter
1 cup brown sugar packed
1 large can of pineapple slices (can use peaches or other canned fruit if you prefer)
½ cup walnut halves (approximate)
Maraschino cherries
1 box yellow cake mix (select one asking for water and eggs to be added as the use of the pineapple juice gives the cake a great flavor)

How to assemble:

Drain pineapple and reserve liquid
In a heavy skillet melt butter, add brown sugar and 2 Tablespoons of the pineapple juice

Cook until carmelized

If you plan to bake the cake in another pan, transfer carmel to baking dish pre-sprayed with PAM

Arrange pineapple slices, cherries and nuts in a pleasing design on top of the carmel in the baking dish

Make cake batter according to instructions on the package, substituting the pineapple juice for the water called for. (If there is not enough pineapple juice for the recipe add water to get appropriate measurement)

Pour batter over fruit and carmel

Bake in oven according to instructions on cake mix, usually 350° for about 45 minutes

When cake is done remove from oven and cool for about 15 minutes

Invert cake on a serving plate and cool until serving.

Notes:

Pound Cake

Originally pound cakes were just that, a pound of sugar, eggs, butter and flour with some vanilla added. Now days you can buy pound cakes frozen or fresh or even as a cake mix. This recipe is a modified pound cake and is fun, cheap and tasty. But in looking at this recipe I would call it a three-quarters of a pound cake.

What you need:

3 sticks or 3/4 lb of butter
3 cups sugar
5 large eggs or 6 small eggs
3 cups flour
1 teaspoon vanilla
½ teaspoon lemon extract or 1 teaspoon grated lemon peel
½ teaspoon almond extract
1 cup minus 2 tablespoons of ginger ale or similar soda

How to assemble:

Using a mixer cream butter until it is light and fluffy
Mix in sugar and continue to beat
Add eggs one at a time until batter is smooth
Beat in one cup of flour
Add the extracts and a small amount of ginger ale
Continue beating
Add flour and ginger ale a little at a time until batter is completely
  mixed and smooth
Pour in to 2 loaf pans or one bundt or tube pan which has been
  sprayed with PAM

Bake in a pre-heated 275° oven for 1hour and 45 minutes or until a toothpick inserted in the middle of the cake comes out clean.

Notes:

Pumpkin Cheese Cake

You've heard of Pumpkin Cheese Cake but have you ever made it? This is a wonderful recipe. Try if for a special occasion. A word of warning, this probably won't freeze well because of the way it is constructed with whipped egg whites, but you might test it with a small piece of leftover, if any.

What you need:

1 ½ cups Zwieback crumbs
3 tablespoons sugar
3 tablespoons melted butter

16 oz softened cream cheese
1 cup light cream or evaporated milk
3/4 cup sugar
4 eggs separated
1 cup canned pumpkin
3 tablespoon flour
1 teaspoon vanilla
1 teaspoon cinnamon
½ teaspoon ginger
½ teaspoon nutmeg
1/4 teaspoon salt

1 cup sour cream
2 tablespoons sugar
½ teaspoon vanilla

How to assemble:

9" spring board pan (this recipe will fill this plus, so have a little
    container ready for the overflow)
Combine Zwieback crumbs 3 tablespoons of sugar and the melted
    butter in the pan.
Pack down in the pan bottom and bake at 325° for five minutes
Remove and cool
Spray sides of pan with PAM
In a medium size bowl whip the egg whites to form stiff peaks and
    set aside
Using a mixer beat cream cheese, cream, egg yolks, pumpkin, flour,
    and spices until creamy smooth
Fold the egg whites into the cream cheese mixture
Pour into spring board pan leaving at least ½ inch to the top of the
    pan
Bake at 325° for one hour then remove from oven

Mix sour cream, sugar and vanilla and pour over cheese cake
Bake another 5 minutes
Chill for at least 3 hours before serving

Notes:

Pumpkin Pie

Pumpkin is my favorite pie. Please don't serve me the frozen pumpkin pie or one made with the pre-mixed canned pie filling. Either make it yourself or buy it from a good bakery. Here is the recipe my mother used and I think it's better than the recipe on the pumpkin can. But, then pumpkin pies are like turkey stuffing, unique to each family and your favorite always taste like you remember as a kid.

What you need:

1 9" pie plate with crust (Use either a Pillsbury pre-packaged crust or the Foolproof Crust in this book)
1 16oz can of pumpkin (Or 2 cups of cooked mashed fresh pumpkin)
2 cups of half and half or canned evaporated milk
3 eggs
4 teaspoons Pumpkin Pie spice
½ teaspoon salt
3/4 cup light brown sugar

How to assemble:

Beat the eggs and sugar together
Add the pumpkin and mix well
Add the spice and salt and continue mixing
Slowly blend in the milk
Pour into a prepared pie crust
Bake in a pre-heated oven at 450° for ten minutes
Reduce the heat to 350° and continue baking for about 50 minutes
   or until a knife inserted in the middle comes out clean.
Cool and serve warm or cold with whipped cream.

Optional—Consider sprinkling Nut Crunch Topping made from
pecans on this pie after it has cool slightly—see the recipe in
this book.

Variations:

Substitute 1/4 cup maple syrup and ½ cup packed brown sugar
for the brown sugar and add 1 cup of pecan halves to the pie
before baking it.

Notes:

Josephine Mohney Coates aka Mom, Granny and Jo

Rum Cake

This cake uses a cake mix for a base. Don't be ashamed of cake mixes. I remember the days before cake mixes and I'm here to tell you that many cakes were real duds. Now no one remembers those dry, tough cakes but there were lots of them. Why do you think people invented deserts like trifle? It was to use up cake that was stale and dry and basically inedible. While many of the cakes in this book are from scratch, some like this one are from a box, proudly.

What you need:

Cake:
1 cup chopped walnuts or pecans
1 box 18 ½ oz. Yellow Cake Mix (make sure it requires the addition
     of eggs and water)
1 box 3 3/4 oz vanilla instant pudding mix
4 eggs
½ cup cold water
½ cup light cooking oil
½ cup dark rum (80 proof)
  or:
If you are using a Yellow Cake Mix with pudding already in the
     mix:
     omit the pudding
     use 3 eggs instead of 4
     1/3 cup of oil instead of ½ cup

Glaze:
1/4 lb butter
1/4 cup water

1 cup sugar

½ cup dark rum (80 proof)

How to assemble:

Heat oven to 325°

Spray either a angel food cake pan or a bundt pan with PAM.

Sprinkle nuts in the bottom of the pan.

Mix all cake ingredients together.

Pour into the pan and bake 1 hour.

Cool and then invert on cake plate.

Meanwhile melt butter for glaze in sauce pan.

Stir in water and sugar.

Bring to boil for five minutes stirring constantly.

Remove from fire and stir in the rum.

Prick the top of the cake with a toothpick and spoon glaze evenly
over the top letting it soak in.

Repeat this process until all the glaze is used.

Notes:

Sherry Wine Cake

This is another way to turn a plain box cake into a delight that just seems to melt away. If you're not a drinker don't let the thought of a sherry wine taste put you off. The cake reminds me of eggnog, it's a rich, buttery moist cake and can be served with only a sprinkling of powdered sugar over the top.

What you need:

1 box 18 ½ oz. Yellow Cake Mix (make sure it requires the addition of eggs and water)
1 box 3 3/4 oz vanilla instant pudding mix
4 eggs
3/4 cup light cooking oil
3/4 cup Cream Sherry
1 teaspoon nutmeg
or:
If you are using a Yellow Cake Mix with pudding already in the mix:
  omit the pudding
  use 3 eggs instead of 4
  ½ cup of oil instead of 3/4 cup

How to assemble:

Heat oven to 350°
Spray either a angel food cake pan or a bundt pan with PAM.
Mix all cake ingredients together.

Pour into the pan and bake 1 hour.

Cool and then invert on cake plate.

Sprinkle powdered sugar over the top before serving

Notes:

Steamed Persimmon Pudding

The first year Dave and I were married we were trying to meld our holiday traditions, nervous less any of the family suffer from omission. Christmas dinner was to be the culmination of the day and I was excited about introducing my new family to my traditional flaming pudding. Well the day went exceeding well, the meal was excellent, and finally it was time for dessert. I proudly brought in this pudding, set it on the table and lit it. Nothing. I laughed and said I needed more rum. It still didn't work. I drowned the pudding in rum and only succeeded in lighting the table cloth, which was my grandmother's. The family was in a uproar. For a while they had tried to be supportive but finally couldn't contain their laughter. The pudding tasted good as it should have seeing it was probably about 100 proof by the time I served it. In subsequent years I finally got the flaming process down, but it was too late, they all remember the failure. Don't worry, I intend to explain the flaming process here. Or if you're afraid to try it, serve it warm with whipped cream or ice cream.

What you need:

1 cup persimmon pulp, pureed. Fresh or frozen, thawed is okay.
2 teaspoons baking soda
½ cup butter or margarine, room temperature
1 ½ cups sugar
2 eggs
2 tablespoons dark rum
1 tablespoon fresh lemon juice
1 cup flour
1 teaspoon cinnamon
½ teaspoon salt

2/3 cup coarsely chopped pecans

How to assemble:

Heat oven to 350° (While this is a steamed pudding, I find it easier to cook in the oven, it seems to make no difference in the finished pudding.) Spray two pudding or cake molds with PAM and set aside.

Add the baking soda to the persimmon puree, stir well and set aside.

Cream butter with sugar in large bowl until light and fluffy.

Beat in eggs, rum and lemon juice.

Add flour, cinnamon and salt and mix well.

Stir in the persimmon puree, don't worry if you find it has gelled.

Add the pecans.

Pour into the molds. (Remember that this is a rich dessert served after a festive meal so you will be serving small pieces. Divide the batter in the molds appropriate to the number you will serve but don't fill the molds more than 2/3's full.)

Seal the molds by snapping the pudding cover on or covering very tightly with foil. If you are using a mold with a tube in the middle make sure the foil fits tightly around the tube but the top of the tube is open so steam can circulate freely through the mold.

Place the molds in a large roasting pan bottom, or baking dish and place in the oven.

Add a couple of inches of boiling water to the pan and cook for about 2 hours.

Add more boiling water during the cooking if necessary.

After two hours carefully remove one pudding and remove foil.

WATCH OUT THAT YOU DON'T BURN YOURSELF WITH THE TRAPPED STEAM.

When the pudding is done it will be a rich, dark brown, and when you insert a toothpick it comes out clean.

If you need to return the pudding to cook longer make sure it is sealed tight again to prevent the build up of condensation on the pudding. If you do have condensation on the pudding, blot carefully with paper towel.

When the pudding is done remove from the oven and uncover. Let cool about twenty minutes then invert on serving plate. When completely cooled cover with plastic wrap and store in the refrigerator or freezer until serving time

How to serve:

This pudding needs to be served warm. So I remove it from the refrigerator prior to cooking dinner. Just before serving I warm it in the microwave. Meanwhile I prepare to flame it by selecting the liquor. I use rum (at least 80 proof) because that is the flavor I cooked with. I warm about a 1/4 cup of rum, careful not to let it boil. You could do this in the microwave. Then I spoon it over the pudding, light the pudding and take it to the table flaming. An alternative way is to take the pudding to the table, then come in with the sauce dish of warmed liquor, light the liquor and pour it over the pudding at the table. Serve with either ice cream or whipped cream for a truly memorable dessert.

By the way, this freezes so well, if I have a lot of persimmons I make these, freeze them and give them away to neighbors and friends for Christmas tokens.

Notes:

Grandma Janet, Dave and Gayle
at our first Christmas dinner.

Strawberry-Rhubarb Pie

I think I told you that Dave Limp, our son-in-law, makes wonderful pies. This is one of his favorites which his Grandmother Gladys made for his family when they went to visit her in Milford, Illinois. This old fashioned pie immediately makes you think of sunny, warm summer days, and big family pot lucks. Now days it's hard to find rhubarb unless you know someone who grows it. When I was growing up Mr. Anderson, who lived down the block, had a crop of rhubarb every year. He always provided us stalks to chew on, all the kids loved the tart sour taste. I'm sorry to say I never had it in a pie until I was grown. So if you find rhubarb at the Farmers' Market or in your grocery store, try this pie yourself and create a new family favorite.

What you need:

Pastry for double crust 9-inch pie (See recipe Dave Limp's Fantastic Pie Crust in this section)
2 ½ cups fresh rhubarb, cut 1/4 inch thick
2 ½ cups fresh strawberries thickly sliced
1 cup sugar
1/4 cup cornstarch
1/4 teaspoon ground nutmeg
2 teaspoons sugar (for crust)

How to assemble:

Combine sugar, cornstarch and nutmeg, stirring until blended
Stir in fruit.
Spoon mixture into pastry shell.

Arrange top crust, flute edges and trim excess crust
Sprinkle top of pastry with 2 teaspoons sugar
Bake in a pre-heated oven at 425 ° for 15 minutes.
Reduce heat to 350° and bake 30 more minutes or until crust is
    browned.

Notes:

You can cook this filling on top of the stove and serve it with
your dinner. Knott's Berry Farm used to serve Strawberry-Rhubarb
sauce with their famous fried chicken dinner.

Sweet Potato Casserole

This recipe came from my cousin "Little Gayle." She was named after me and as children we looked a lot alike. I used to babysit for her and her brothers. Her parents, Aunt Clara and Uncle Bruce and their kids were close to my parents. During the 50's we shared holiday and weekly poker parties.

Little Gayle moved to Tennessee with her husband so I hadn't seen much of her in the past thirty years but when Uncle Bernie turned 80 everyone showed up in Kalamazoo to help him celebrate and there again Gayle met Little Gayle. Sadly, Little Gayle died suddenly the following year so we'll never have another reunion but she will be remembered by us all and for more than this recipe.

You've heard of Sweet Potato Pie, well this casserole is similar to the filling for that pie. It is really a desert pudding and should be served with a little whipped cream.

What you need:

3 cups of cooked, mashed sweet potatoes
½ cup brown sugar, packed
½ cup butter
2 eggs
1 teaspoon vanilla
1 teaspoon cinnamon
½ cup chopped walnuts or pecans

How to assemble:

Mix all the ingredients except the nuts together
Pour into a greased baking dish

Sprinkle the nuts over the top
Bake in a 350° oven for 30 minutes
Serve warm or chilled with ice cream or whipped cream

Notes:

Tapioca Pudding Parfait

When I was cooking for the family we always had to serve dessert and so we made pudding often. At that time there wasn't a profusion of boxed puddings like today, so mostly we made puddings from scratch. Tapioca was always one of my favorites, but one day I was poking through the cupboards and found a can of sour cherries and lo and behold this desert emerged. When I moved to San Francisco this was my roommates' favorite. When Dave and I married it was certainly one of the family's favorites. So here it is for you to try yourself. By the way, I've heard people say that they didn't like Tapioca Pudding and I'll admit that if you've ever been served the gluey, rubbery kind I can understand it. But I've never found anyone who didn't enjoy this light, frothy pudding.

What you need:

Cherry filling:
1 can water packed sour cherries
1 cup sugar
4 tablespoons corn starch
1/4 teaspoon red food coloring
3 drops almond extract

Pudding:
3 tablespoons tapioca
5 tablespoons sugar
1/8 teaspoon salt

1 3/4 cups milk
3 eggs, separated
1 teaspoon vanilla

How to assemble:

Cherry Filling:
Drain the cherries, reserving liquid
In a sauce pan combine corn starch, sugar and 3/4 cup of liquid
    from cherries (if liquid does not make 3/4 cup add water)
Bring to a gentle boil and cook until mixtures thickens to a pleasing
    consistency.
Cook for one minute
Remove from heat and add cherries, food coloring and almond extract
Stir well and let cool

Pudding:
Beat egg whites until foamy
Gradually add 3 tablespoons of sugar and continue to beat until
    soft peaks form
Set egg whites aside
In a large sauce pan mix milk, 3 tablespoons of sugar, tapioca, salt
    and egg yolks and let stand one minute
Cook tapioca mix on a medium heat, stirring constantly until it
    comes to a full boil.
Continue cooking for about 8 minutes making sure it doesn't scorch.
Remove from heat and gradually add to the egg white mixture,
    stirring quickly until just blended
Stir in the vanilla

Serving:
Select parfait or pretty wine glasses
Spoon some cherry filling into bottom of glass
Spoon pudding on top of cherry filling
Add more cherry filling and pudding in layers until glass is full.
Chill until serving (at least 1 ½ hours)

Notes:

In a hurry, no reason you can't buy a can of Cherry Pie filling instead of making your own. I like the little tartness in the cherries when I make my own but I have used the canned filling in a pinch.

Teresa's Chocolate Pudding Cake

Most of you know that Teresa is my little sister, she came eleven years after my youngest brother and was raised amidst her niece and nephews. Because of that she frequently feels left out when we tell stories of our childhood. She had a whole other experience growing up but now that she's adult and on equal footing with the rest of us its amazing how alike we are in many ways. I'm not ashamed to admit that she provided me an excellent alternative way to cook turkey and of course this cake. The best way to serve this cake is warm, spooned over ice cream. Time the baking so it comes out of the oven when you sit down for the meal and it will be a perfect temperature to serve for desert. This serves 4 to 6 but if you have big eaters, double it.

What you need:

1 cup all purpose flour
3/4 cup granulated sugar
1 cup brown sugar, packed
1/4 cup + 2 tablespoons unsweetened cocoa
2 teaspoons baking powder
1/4 teaspoon salt
2 tablespoons vegetable oil
½ cup milk
1 teaspoon vanilla
1 3/4 cups very hot water
ice cream to serve

How to assemble:

Heat oven to 350°

In an ungreased 9 x 9 x 2 baking pan mix flour, baking powder, salt, 2 tablespoon cocoa

Add milk, vegetable oil and vanilla and stir well

Spread evenly over pan

Mix the brown sugar and 1/4 cup cocoa together and sprinkle over the batter

Pour very hot water on top

Bake for about 40 minutes

Cool about 15 or 20 minutes

Spoon over dishes of ice cream

Notes:

When you put this together don't worry about the hot water floating on top of the batter. You didn't do anything wrong. Trust me, it will be wonderful.

I love nuts and if you do, mix some with the brown sugar and cocoa you sprinkle over the top of the batter, before you put the hot water on. It's great.

Teresa and her husband, Ken.

Thelma's Coffee Cake

During the years we lived on the Highway in Long Beach, my mother wasn't working. With five kids, who had time? But she would get up and cook hot cereal, listen to her radio show, The Breakfast Club, and see that we all got off to school on time. Once in a while she would surprise us by baking this coffee cake that came from her friend, Thelma.

Thelma Anselmo was one of the woman in the PTA at Whittier Grammar School. Those women formed a club that met monthly for about 30 years. They competed with each other to have kooky themes for these meetings and they had a lot of fun. Over the years they all knew about everyone's lives, families and their stories. They became like family.

What you need:

2 cups flour
½ teaspoon salt
1 cup brown sugar (packed)
3/4 cup white sugar
1 teaspoon nutmeg
3/4 cup oil
1 cup buttermilk or sour milk (you can make sour milk by adding 1 tablespoon of lemon juice or vinegar to your milk and letting set five minutes before using—remember to remove 1 tablespoon of milk to make sure the measurement is right)
1 egg
1 teaspoon soda
1 teaspoon baking powder
½ cup chopped nuts

How to assemble:

Mix the first 6 ingredients well
Remove ½ cup of mixed ingredients and set aside
Add buttermilk, egg, soda and baking powder and mix well
Pour batter into a greased square cake pan
Mix reserved ingredients with the chopped nuts
Sprinkle mixture evenly over the top of the cake
Bake in a preheated oven at 350° for 30 minutes or until cakes
    springs back when pressed with your finger
Serve warm.

Notes:

Tomato Soup Cake

That's right, tomato soup. And its delicious. Just the thing when you need to bake something different but great. And won't you love telling everyone what is in it? Don't worry they'll believe you because it is tomato soup red but otherwise unrelated to what you'd expect tomato soup to taste like. This is a real cake, that means it's not made from a cake mix but it is rather simple to make.

What you need:

2 round Pyrex cake pans
1 cup sugar
½ cup butter or margarine, room temperature
1 can tomato soup
1 teaspoon baking soda (dissolve it in the soup)
2 cups flour
2 teaspoons baking powder
1 teaspoon cinnamon
½ teaspoon nutmeg
½ teaspoon cloves
1 cup chopped nut meats (optional)
1 cup raisins (optional)

How to assemble:

If you have decided to use the raisins pour boiling water over them. Let them set in the hot water for 10 minutes, then drain and dry them by patting off excess water with a paper towel. This will give you plump juicy raisins.
Set oven at 350°

Get pans ready by spraying with PAM, cutting out wax paper circles to put on bottom of the pan, then spraying with PAM over the paper.

Cream the butter and sugar together.

Add the tomato soup right from the can with only the baking soda added.

Slowly add the flour, baking powder and spices, mixing thoroughly

Add the raisins and/or nuts

Pour ½ of the batter in each of the cake pans

Bake for approximately 30 minutes or until a toothpick inserted in the center comes out clean.

Remove from the oven for 10 minutes then turn out on a rack to thoroughly cool.

This can be frosted with your favorite icing but I use Cream Cheese Icing (see recipe) and decorate it with nuts.

Notes:

The Ultimate Cheese Cake

Mom got this recipe from her friend Pauline (one of the women from her club) and made it for years to everyone's delight. But one time I made a mistake in making it and loved the change. That encouraged me to experiment further and now I defy you to find or make a better cheese cake than a variation of this one.

Gayle's Rule for Freezing Applies Here:
Anything Sara Lee Can Freeze, So Can I.

This cake freezes so well that frequently I'll make two, one for the freezer. Or, if only part of the cake is eaten freeze the rest for another occasion. There are three steps in making this cake, the crust, the cheese cake and the topping. I have numbered them so you can keep your place.

Caution: Don't try to reduce calories by using low calorie cream cheese or substituting cottage cheese for cream cheese. If you're watching your calories serve smaller pieces and enjoy the real thing.

What you need:

large spring board pan 9-10 inches in diameter, sprayed with PAM

1. 2 cups of cookie or graham cracker crumbs
    1/4 cup of melted butter or margarine

2. 18 oz. cream cheese at room temperature
    3 eggs
    1 cup + 2 tablespoons of sugar

2/3 teaspoon of fresh lemon juice
3 teaspoons vanilla

3. 1 ½ cups of sour cream
    5 tablespoons of sugar
    1 ½ teaspoons vanilla

How to assemble:

1. *Crust:*

Use graham crackers, chocolate wafer cookies or vanilla cookies and turn to crumbs. Go ahead, do all of them, any amount over two cups can be frozen for another day.

Mix 2 cups of crumbs with the melted butter and pack tightly in the bottom of the springboard pan. Do not go up the sides, it's too much crust.

Bake in a 350° oven for ten minutes, remove and let cool.

2. *Cheese Cake:*

Blend cream cheese, eggs, sugar, lemon juice and vanilla until smooth and creamy. (Hint; I use the Cuisinart in two batches then combine and mix well for easy, fast mixing)

Pour over crust in springboard pan

Bake at 350° for 1 hour, until top is crusty, slightly split and the sides are drawing away from the pan.

Remove from oven and cool 10 minutes.

3. *Topping:*

While cake is cooling combine the sour cream with the 5 tablespoons of sugar and the 1 ½ teaspoons of vanilla.

When cake has cooled for 10 minutes pour topping over cheese cake and spread it evenly.

Bake another 10 minutes.

Chill 3 to 5 hours before serving.

Try some variations:

Chocolate Marble Cheese Cake

Make crust from 2 cups of chocolate wafer cookies and add ½ cup chopped pecans to chocolate cookie crust.

Pour ½ cake batter in the pan, then pour 1/4 cup of Hershey's Chocolate syrup on top, pour in the rest of the batter. Take a table knife and carefully swirl it through the batter, make sure you don't hit the crust on the bottom.

Topping on this can be hot fudge sauce or use the sour cream topping and decorate with shaved chocolate when chilled.

Spiced Apple Cheese Cake

For spiced apple cheese cake I add ½ cup finely chopped walnuts and ½ teaspoon of cinnamon to the crust of vanilla wafer cookie crumbs.

For the cake, peel, core and slice 2 or 3 tart cooking apples

Toss the slices in sugar, cinnamon, cloves and a pinch of nutmeg. Lay 1/3 apple slices on crust, pour 1/3 cake batter on them, lay down another layer, add 1/3 cake batter and more apples, finishing with last of batter.

Use sour cream topping.

Blueberry Cheese Cake

For blueberry cheese cake I add ½ cup finely chopped walnuts to either graham cracker or vanilla cookie crust.

When the batter is complete, fold in 1 cup of fresh blueberries. (If these have been frozen, be sure to defrost and drain the berries before using or it will effect your baking time.)

Try your own.

Use your imagination and don't forget to share the successes with the rest of us.

Notes:

Vanya's Strawberry Dream Cake

Vanya and I met in the 7ᵗʰ grade at Franklin Junior High School and have remained good friends since. While I moved to San Francisco, she moved to Atlanta and subsequently, San Diego. Vanya has many talents but one is that she is a gourmet cook. She has infinite patience; she has taken numerous cooking courses and she is a serious cook. Maybe it was all those years her family owned and operated restaurants or maybe she just has the talent. Most the meals she serves I just enjoy as if I was at a restaurant, knowing I don't have the ambition to attempt to duplicate her recipes. But once in a while she serves something that inspires me to try. This is such a recipe. It looks, tastes and is dreamy.

What you need:

1 package of white cake mix (pick one requiring eggs and water)
1 small package of Strawberry Jello
2 tablespoons of flour
4 eggs
½ cup water
½ box of frozen, sliced strawberries (thawed)
3/4 cup cooking oil

How to assemble:

Mix together the cake mix, Jello and flour
Stir in the eggs, water, strawberries and juice and oil
Mix thoroughly
Pour into a sheet cake pan

Bake in a pre-heated oven at 350° for approximately 30-40 minutes or until a toothpick inserted in the middle comes out clean.
Remove from the oven and cool
Frost this cake with Strawberry Butter Icing found in this book.

Notes:

Veenie's Carrot Cake

Veenie is my sister-in-law, Linda's, mother and she became a member of our family the first time we met her. Veenie had more funny stories to tell than anyone I know, except her daughter. Make this cake and then serve it up at a good story telling session, everyone will enjoy it.

What you need:

4 eggs
1 ½ cups vegetable oil
2 cups sugar
2 cups flour
1 ½ teaspoons baking soda
2 teaspoons baking powder
1 teaspoon salt
2 teaspoons cinnamon
2 cups grated raw carrots
1 can (8 ½ oz) drained crushed pineapple
1 cup chopped nuts (optional)

How to assemble:

Beat together the eggs, oil and sugar until thick and creamy
Stir in the carrots and pineapple
In a separate bowl mix the flour, soda, baking powder, salt and
    cinnamon together
Slowly add the flour mixture to the batter, stirring well

Add the nuts

Pour into sheet pan or layer pans which have been sprayed with PAM

Bake at 350°for approximately 50 minutes or until a toothpick
inserted in the middle of the cake comes out clean.

Cool, then frost with Cream Cheese Icing—see recipe in this book.

Notes:

Velma's Date Pudding

When I was copying the recipes for Emma Mohney's section I found this recipe in it. Mom had written it down in 1954. Her handwriting resembles her mother's so closely I wouldn't have known the difference if she hadn't dated it.

Velma was another member of that famous club with no name that my Mom belonged to. And that is where Mom got this recipe. She served this several times at family meals, it's rich and different.

What you need:

2 cups dates, coarsely chopped
2 cups nuts, coarsely chopped
4 eggs
2 cups sugar
2 teaspoons baking powder
1/4 cup sifted flour
1/4 cup milk

How to assemble:

Beat eggs till frothy
Add sugar and beat in
Sift baking powder with flour
Add flour to eggs
Add dates and nuts
Pour into 13 x 9 x 2 greased pan

Bake 325° 50 minutes

Serve warm with whipped cream

Notes:

Cream Cheese Icing

This is a great icing for many cakes. I use it on Carrot Cake, which is traditional, and Tomato Soup Cake, and on a rare occasion even on the Raisin Cake. Try your own combinations.

What you need:

1/4 cup butter or margarine
4 oz. cream cheese
½ teaspoon vanilla
½ lb powdered sugar

How to Assemble:

Cream the butter and cream cheese together.
Mix in the vanilla
Add the powdered sugar slowly, mixing well. If the icing is too
    stiff to spread easily add milk until you reach the right
    consistency.

This is enough to frost a sheet cake, double the recipe for a layer
    cake.

Notes:

Fudge Frosting

This frosting comes from Aunt Kate's Brownie recipe but it is too good to restrict to only one use. Would you like a lemon layer cake with fudge frosting? What about a chocolate cake with fudge between the layers? Now you're getting the idea.

Don't feel that boxed cakes require boxed or canned frosting. The mixing and matching is what makes each cook's work unique.

What you need:

1 ½ cups sugar
6 tablespoons of margerine (or butter)
6 tablespoons milk
1 cup of semi-sweet chocolate chips
½ teaspoon of vanilla

How to assemble:

Place sugar, butter and milk in a 1 ½ quart sauce pan and bring to a boil
Boil one minute stirring constantly then remove from the flame
Beat in the chocolate chips and the vanilla
Continue beating until mixture is creamy
Frost cake with a thin layer of frosting, smoothing with a large knife. You make need to keep pan setting in hot water while frosting the cake to keep the fudge liquid enough to spread.
This icing will harden to a fudge like consistency so keep that in mind when using it.

Notes:

Mock Marshmallow Frosting

Sometimes a cake needs more than icing that came out of a can or a box. When that happens try this little number and see what it does to a plain, old cake. I got this recipe from a girl I met when I first came to San Francisco. I don't remember the cake recipe but I loved the frosting and have used it ever since.

What you need:

5 tablespoons flour
1 cup milk
1 cup sugar
1 cup butter or oleo (two cubes) softened
1 teaspoon vanilla

How to assemble:

Place the flour in a pan
Add milk, first just enough to make a paste and then slowly add the rest of the milk until no lumps are present
Add sugar and then cook the mixture, stirring constantly until it boils and thickens
Remove from heat and set aside to cool
Meanwhile, beat butter until almost white
Slowly add cooled mixture, continuing to beat until frosting is light and fluffy
Add vanilla, give it a last stirring and frost your cake.

Notes:

Seven Minute Icing

There was a time you couldn't buy frosting in a can or a box and so you had to make your own. This was very popular but I think that you can't make this on a rainy day as the humidity does something to prevent the icing from whipping up properly. Try it on a sunny day and see what you think.

What you need:

1 ½ cups sugar
2 egg whites
½ cup water
½ teaspoon vanilla

How to assemble:

Put the sugar, egg whites and water in the top of a double boiler
    and heat to boiling.
Add vanilla
Beat mixture until cool and soft peaks form
Ice the cake
Decorate if desired with coconut or sprinkles

Notes:

Strawberry Butter Frosting

This icing is perfect for Vanya's Strawberry Dream Cake but it is equally wonderful on vanilla or yellow cup cakes. It makes a plain cake very special.

What you need:

½ cup butter
1 lb powdered sugar
½ pkg frozen strawberries (thawed)
½ teaspoon vanilla

How to assemble:

Beat butter until light and fluffy
Mix the sugar, strawberries and vanilla together
Beat sugar mixture slowly into the butter
Continue to beat until frosting is the consistency of whipped cream
Frost the cake.

Notes:

Walnut Butter Icing

This is the icing used for Aunt Nell's special Torte Cake but it is too good to reserve only for that cake. It will help make any cake special but remember that it needs to be refrigerated.

What you need:

1 cup milk
1 cup walnuts, finely grated
1 cup of sweet butter
2 cups of powdered sugar

Boil the milk and pour over the ground walnuts
Let cool to room temperature
Cream the butter
Add the powdered sugar slowly and beat until mixture is almost
  white.
Add nut/milk mixture slowly and continue beating until the
  mixture is now the consistency of whipped cream.

Notes:

Emma's Secrets

Emma's family amidst their grapes. Left to right are Jake (Pop), Emma, Phiney (Josephine), Bud (Dillis), Flo (Florence), and Nellie (Nell) Mohney. Probably taken around 1920.

CONTENTS

Who Was Emma Mohney?

Emma Lewis, my grandmother, married Jake Mohney I believe somewhere around Punxsutawney, Pennsylvania about 1905. A few year later the couple moved to Vicksburg, Michigan, to farm. Jake's two brothers had farms there and one of the farms is still owned by my cousin, Grace Mohney. Emma and Jake lived and farmed while raising their four children. It must have been a hard life with no electricity or indoor plumbing. The children, Nell, Florence, Bud (Dillis) and Phinnie (Josephine) all had to work along with their parents.

Jake farmed at least three properties at various times. He would grow whatever crop would get them some income. And of course there was always a garden and probably chickens and some farm animals. My mother told stories about a goose that kept her imprisoned on the porch and the baby lamb she once had as a pet.

Emma's little brown book was the notebook she used to jot down recipes given her by neighbors and friends. Ingredients were hard to come by and too precious to waste, so the recipes were carefully guarded and used over and over.

Emma died when my mother was in her last year of high school. She had some kind of kidney disease and was sent to a big hospital for treatment. She didn't come back.

My mother used Emma's notebook throughout her life. When Mom died, I took the now fragile, barely legible notebook and promised to copy the recipes for the rest of the family.

Here they are. I haven't attempted to translate them as I think they are more effective as they are written. It was quite difficult to copy them, I used magnifying glasses, pasted torn pieces together like jigsaw puzzles and even had to guess in a few cases. I have taken the liberty of reordering the recipes to better describe what they are. But rest assured that I have given you all the information that was recorded in the book.

I hope you have fun with these recipes. Figuring out how much butter equals an egg or is the size of a walnut and identifying the amount a milking spoon contains of vanilla might take a little more imagination.

A few of the recipes I have not copied in this section as it turns out that I have already put them in the book, not realizing their source.

- Mrs. Utter's Christmas Fruit Cake = Mom's Raisin Cake
- Mrs. Quigley's Tomato Soup Cake = Tomato Soup Cake
- Mrs. Dicken's Johnnie Cake = Johnnie Cake

Many of these recipes use sour milk. At that time there was little refrigeration so milk and cream turned sour regularly and recipes using the sour milk were popular. You can make sour milk by adding a tablespoon of vinegar or lemon juice to a cup of sweet milk. You'll probably notice that when using sour milk the recipe always calls for baking soda.

There were no instructions with any of the recipes but I'm sure that was because every one then knew how to cook the basics, a cake, cookies, ice cream, a pie and all they needed was the proportions and the ingredients. So here they are. I hope you will try some of these recipes and you will share the results with other members of the family. Consulting on a recipe is a great excuse to call a cousin or an aunt and generally stay in touch.

Aunt Ella's Bush
(Dill Pickles)

Soak over night in strong salt water
In a.m. put into jar
Cut up dill and put into jars
Put horseradish in jars
Boil 4 quarts of vinegar with alum and 1 cup salt
Let cool
Pour over pickles and seal

Notes:

Chunk Pickles

Soak in strong salt water for 3 days
Soak in clear water for 3 days
Cut into chunks
Boil for 2 hours in very weak vinegar with 1 oz of Alum

Syrup:

3 pints vinegar
3 lbs white sugar
1 oz whole allspice
1 oz stick cinnamon
1 oz celery seed

Put chunks in syrup
Let come to a boil

Notes:

Corn Relish

1 dozen ears of corn
4 large onions
1 cabbage
1 tablespoon salt
1 tablespoon dry mustard
1 teaspoon timeric powder
1 teaspoon flour
1 tablespoon celery seed
1 ½ quart vinegar
1 cup sugar
2 red peppers

Notes:

Hilda's Mincemeat

4 lbs lean beef
Cook in small amount of water for 3 ½ hours
Remove gristle and bone
When cold put through food grinder
Reduce liquid to 1 pint
1 ½ lbs suet
4 teaspoons salt
5 quarts chopped apples
2 lbs sugar
2 lbs currants
½ lb citron
3 oranges
3 lemons
1 quart boiled cider
4 teaspoons cinnamon
2 teaspoons mace
1 teaspoon cloves
Cook 30 minutes
Makes 8 quarts

Notes:

Hilda's Mixed Mustard Pickles

1 quart small cukes
1 quart large cukes, cubed
1 quart small onions
1 cauliflower
1 diced muskmellon*
Cover with salt water over night
Drain in a.m.

Dressing:
2 quarts vinegar
4 cups brown sugar
2 cups flour
6 tablespoons dry mustard
1 teaspoon timeric
Stir with cold vinegar
Then add to boiling liquid
Drop in cukes
Let come to boil
Seal

*My mother frequently called cantaloupe muskmellon

Notes:

Mrs. Barn's Mustard Pickles

Aug, 1921

To 1 gallon vinegar:

1 cup sugar
1 cup salt
1 cup dry mustard
1 leaf powdered alum horseradish root

Notes:

Pickled Apples or Peaches

4 lbs white sugar
1 pt vinegar
This makes 1 gallon of pickles
Every three days for three times pour off syrup
Heat and put over fruit again

Notes:

Sauerkraut

Mrs. Van Kreaken
Aug. 11, 1932

Put sliced cabbage in quart jars
Put in 1 teaspoon salt
Fill jar with cold water
Tighten cover

Notes:

To Can Beets

1 ½ cups vinegar
½ cup sugar
2 teaspoons salt
Let come to a boil
Enough for two quarts

Notes:

Blanche's Fruit Cake

1 cup raisins chopped fine
1 cup sugar
½ cup water boil slowly 5 minutes
1 large tablespoon butter
Cool
1 egg beaten
2 cups flour
2 teaspoons baking powder
3 tablespoons nut meats
1 teaspoon nutmeg
1 teaspoon cinnamon

Frosting:

1 ½ cups powdered sugar
butter the size of a walnut
Mix well together
Add beaten yolk of egg
Add flavors

Notes:

Blanche's Nut Bread

1 egg beaten in bowl
3/4 cup sugar
1 1/4 cup sour milk
3 cups flour
4 teaspoons baking powder
3/4 teaspoon of soda
1 teaspoon salt
1 cup nut meats
Bake 1 hour in moderate oven

Notes:

Blanches' Sour Cream Cake

May 11, 1923

1 cup sugar
2 eggs
salt
(Beat real good)
1 cup sour cream
1 level teaspoon soda
scant 2 cups flour
scant 1 teaspoon baking powder
vanilla
(This makes 3 nice layers)

Notes:

Chocolate Cake

1 cup sugar
1 egg
1 tablespoon butter
1 cup sour milk
½ teaspoon soda
½ cup cocoa in hot water
2 cups flour
1 ½ teaspoons baking powder
flavoring

Notes:

Coffee Cake

1 egg
2 tablespoons sugar
1 tablespoon melted butter
1 cup milk
1 ½ cups flour
1 teaspoon baking powder

Put butter, brown sugar and cinnamon over top of cake and bake.

Notes:

Hilda's Angel Food Cake

June 21, 1924

whites of 8 large or 9 medium size eggs
1 1/4 cups sugar
1 cup flour
½ teaspoon cream of tarter
pinch of salt added to egg whites before whipping
flavors to taste

Sift flour 5 times
Sift sugar 5 times
Before breaking eggs
Bake about 45 minutes

Notes:

Hilda's Molasses Cake

1 cup sugar
½ cup lard
2 eggs
1 cup cold coffee
1 cup molasses
2 cups flour (*May be 3 cups, difficult to read*)
1 teaspoon soda, cinnamon
Pinch of ginger
Salt

Notes:

Mrs. Otto Barnes Chocolate Cake

1 cup sugar
4 tablespoons butter
3 tablespoons cocoa
1 egg
1 cup milk
1 1/4 cup flour
1 teaspoon soda
1 teaspoon vanilla
Sift flour, cocoa and soda together and add last
Makes a 2 layer cake

Notes:

Mrs. Spires' 3 Egg Angel Cake

3/4 cup sugar
2 /3 cup milk
3 egg whites
1/8 teaspoon salt
1 cup pastry flour
2 teaspoons baking powder
½ teaspoon cream of tartar
1 teaspoon vanilla

Heat milk and sugar just to boil
Add salt to egg whites and beat till stiff
Add hot syrup slowly to egg whites beat continually
Let cool
Sift together 5 times flour, cream of tartar and baking powder
Fold flour into egg mixture
Pour into ungreased angel tin
Bake in moderate oven 350° about 30 minutes

Notes:

Mrs. Spires' Gold Cake

3 tablespoons shortening
3/4 cup sugar
3 egg yolks (beat)
1 teaspoon vanilla
1 ½ cups flour
3 teaspoons baking powder
½ cup milk

375° for 35 minutes or 25 minutes for shallow pan

Notes:

Mrs. Tilberry's Bread Sponge Cake

I don't understand the Bread Sponge listed in this cake but it was very clear that it was 1 cup of Bread Sponge. On the same page is a recipe for Sponge Cake. Do you make this cake with leftover Sponge Cake? If anyone figures this out, please let me know.

1 ½ cups sugar
½ cup lard
1 cup raisins
1 egg
½ cup sour milk
1 cup bread sponge
1 teaspoon cinnamon
1 teaspoon cloves
½ teaspoon nutmeg
1 teaspoon soda
flour to make rather stiff batter

Notes:

Mrs. Utter's Molasses Cake

1 cup brown sugar
½ cup lard
1 egg
½ cup molasses (little less)
Spices—cinnamon, cloves, nutmeg, ginger, about a teaspoon except
    nutmeg 1/4 teaspoon of it
2 cups sifted flour (measure after sifting)
1 cup boiling water
1 teaspoon soda
1 teaspoon baking powder
Batter real thin
Bake slow

Notes:

Mrs. (Dr.) Young's 2 Egg Cake

1 cup sugar
2 eggs in cup, fill cup with milk
1 3/4 cup flour
2 teaspoons baking powder
4 tablespoons melted butter vanilla

Notes:

Nell's Applesauce Cake

1 cup sugar
1 cup unsweetened applesauce
1 teaspoon soda
½ teaspoon baking powder
½ cup raisins
2 cups flour
1 teaspoon nutmeg pinch cloves
½ cup shortening

Notes:

Ora's Molasses Cake

1 egg
1 cup sugar
½ cup molasses
1 cup coffee
5 tablespoons melted shortening
1 teaspoon soda
½ teaspoon spices flour for soft batter
(raisins if desired)

Notes:

Orillas Graham Bread

1cup sugar
1 egg
1 ½ cups sour milk
1 teaspoon soda
½ teaspoon salt
2 cups graham flour raisins

Notes:

Short Cake

2 cups flour
salt
3 teaspoons baking powder
sift together
large tablespoon lard
1 cup sour milk
small pinch of soda
pour into pans
bake ½ hour

Notes:

Sponge Cake

2 eggs
1 cup sugar pinch salt
1 cup flour
½ cup boiling water
vanilla
beat well

Notes:

Upside Down Cake

Annabell's
Nov. 2, 1931

4 tablespoons melted butter
1 cup brown sugar
put in pie tin and melt together
place pineapple slices on pan

Batter:
1 cup sugar
1/4 cup butter
1 egg
½ cup milk
1 ½ cups flour
1 teaspoon vanilla
1 teaspoon baking powder

Notes:

Chocolate Drop Fudge

Lydia Murray's

2 ½ cups sugar
cocoa to color the sugar
3/4 cup milk
cook slowly to form soft ball
pour into 3 plates
put chunk of butter and ½ teaspoon of vanilla on each plate
beat with a knife and drop on oil paper

Notes:

One of the farms in Lawton, Michigan where Emma and Jake lived while raising their kids.

Divinity Fudge

2 cups sugar
½ cup Karo Syrup
1 cup water
cook until it "hairs"
pour over beaten whites of 2 eggs
add flavor and nuts

Notes:

Fudge

2 cups sugar
1 cup milk
butter size of an egg
1 cup cocoa
cook until it hairs
flavor

Notes:

Fudge Strips

½ cup butter
1 cup sugar
1 cup flour
1 cup nut meats
2 tablespoons cocoa
vanilla

Notes:

Peanut Butter Fudge

2 cups of brown sugar
½ cup of cream
boil until it forms soft ball in cold water
let cool
add 2 tablespoon peanut butter
beat until smooth

Notes:

Penoche

2 cups brown sugar
½ cup sweet cream
1 cup nut meats flavor

Notes:

Sea Foam

3 cups brown sugar
1/4 cup water
boil until brittle when dropped in cold water
pour over beaten whites of 2 eggs
add nut meats

Notes:

Sugar Taffy

1 lb sugar
½ glass cold water
add 1 teaspoon cream or tartar
lump of butter size of hickory nut
1 teaspoon vinegar
do not stir at all
boil slow 25 minutes
pour on buttered pans
pour flavoring over it
pull taffy until very white

Notes:

Aunt Lydia's Orange Cookies

2 cups sugar
1 cup shortening cream well
3 eggs
grated rind and juice of 2 oranges
1 cup sour milk
1 teaspoon soda
6 cups flour
2 teaspoons baking powder
drop big teaspoons on pan in hot oven

Icing:
grated rind and juice of one orange
mix in 1 box of powdered sugar (1lb)
spread on cookies

Notes:

Aunty Dye's Cookies

1 cup brown sugar
1 cup white sugar
1 cup lard salt
2 eggs well beaten
½ teaspoon nutmeg
½ teaspoon soda
2/3 cup cold water
2 teaspoon baking powder
4-6 cups flour to make soft dough bake in quick oven

Notes:

Blanche's Oatmeal Cookies

1 cup sugar
1 cup shortening
pinch of salt
2 eggs
½ cup sour milk
1 teaspoon soda
1 2/3 cups oatmeal
2 1/3 cups flour
1 cup raisins, chopped

Notes:

Carrie's Doughnuts

April 9, 1920

1 cup sugar
1 ½ cup milk
4 large tablespoons lard
1 egg
2 teaspoons baking powder
nutmeg, lemon and ginger
flour

Notes:

Doughnuts

2 cups sugar
2 cups sour milk
2 eggs
salt
2 tablespoon lard
ginger
1 teaspoon soda
1 teaspoon baking powder
flour to make soft dough

Notes:

Drop Molasses Cookies

2/3 cup sugar
½ cup molasses
½ cup lard
1/4 cup hot water
1 teaspoon of soda, ginger & cinnamon
1 egg
salt
3 cups of flour

Notes:

Miss Cory's Hermits

1 cup light brown sugar
½ cup sour milk
½ cup butter or lard
1 egg
pinch of salt
1 cup chopped raisins
1 cup nut meats
little of each, cloves, cinnamon & nutmeg
1 teaspoon soda
1 ½ cups flour

Notes:

Carmel Ice Cream

1 ½ cup brown sugar melted
1 ½ cup white sugar
3/4 cup flour
2 eggs
1 gallon cream

Notes:

Visit in 1994 to Grace Mohney's farm. Jake's brother's farm is still in the Mohney family. Standing is Gracie Mohney and her sister, seated are Gib, his son, Matt, Teresa, Gayle, Connie's daughter, Leslie, and Connie.

My Own Recipe for Carmel Ice Cream

Feb 9 Nell's 23 year birthday

3 cups of melted brown sugar
2 cups white sugar
3 quarts of milk
put in waterless cooker
when boiling add
2/3 cup flour
yolks of 6 eggs beaten smoothly
pinch of salt
strain through sieve
add 2 cans of milk
beat egg whites
add
1 ½ large spoons vanilla (a large milking spoon)

Notes:

Carmel Pudding
(Sherwoods)

2 cups brown sugar
2 cups boiling water
let boil 3 minutes
3 tablespoons cornstarch
butter size of a walnut
pinch of salt
1 cup of coconut or nut meats
serve with whipped cream

Notes:

Cornstarch Pudding

Blanche's
April 11, 1926

1 pint milk, heat quite hot
stir 2 heaping tablespoons of cornstarch, two of sugar and pinch of
   salt with a little milk to a smooth paste
let boil
remove pan
let cool
add vanilla and whites of 3 well beaten eggs into mixture and let
   get ice cold

Second Step:
1 pint milk
beaten yolks of 3 eggs
½ cup sugar pnch of salt let scald

Use this over the White pudding

Notes:

Mrs. Utter's Suet Pudding

2 cups bread crumbs
1 cup cold water
2 cups molasses
1 cup raisins
1 cup flour
1 cup suet
1 teaspoon soda
1 egg
steam 2 hours

Notes:

Suet Pudding

1 cup suet
1 cup molasses
1 cup raisins
1 cup sour milk
salt
2 teaspoons soda
stir suet, molasses and raisins together
dissolve soda in sour milk
add flour to make stiff batter
steam 2 hours

Notes:

Nell's Chop Suey

1 bottle shou (soy) sauce
1 can bean sprouts
1 cup celery chopped
1 cup onion chopped
1 ½ lbs beef or pork diced
fry meat first
add onion and celery
add sauce
add molasses or sugar
simmer
salt and pepper to taste
add sprouts just before serving

Notes:

Nell's Lemon Pie

1 cup sugar
3 tablespoon cornstarch
pinch salt
juice and grated rind of 1 lemon
yolks of 2 eggs
piece of butter
2 cups of boiling water

Notes:

Emma and Jake Mohney with Nellie and Flo, probably taken in 1910 or 1911.